TREES, LEAVES, FLOWERS & SEEDS

A VISUAL ENCYCLOPEDIA OF THE PLANT KINGDOM

TREES, LEAVES, FLOWERS & SEEDS

A VISUAL ENCYCLOPEDIA OF THE PLANT KINGDOM

WRITTEN BY **DR SARAH JOSE**
CONSULTANT **DR CHRIS CLENNETT**

DK DELHI
Senior Editors Anita Kakar, Bharti Bedi, Rupa Rao
Senior Art Editor Shreya Anand
Editor Arpita Dasgupta
Art Editors Baibhav Parida, Debjyoti Mukherjee
Assistant Editor Bipasha Roy
Assistant Art Editors Sifat Fatima, Sanya Jain
Jacket Designer Tanya Mehrotra
Jackets Editorial Coordinator Priyanka Sharma
Senior DTP Designer Harish Aggarwal
DTP Designers Jaypal Chauhan, Ashok Kumar, Vijay Kandwal, Mohammad Rizwan, Vikram Singh, Rakesh Kumar
Senior Picture Researcher Sumedha Chopra
Picture Researchers Aditya Katyal, Vishal Ghavri
Picture Research Manager Taiyaba Khatoon
Managing Jackets Editor Saloni Singh
Pre-production Manager Balwant Singh
Production Manager Pankaj Sharma
Managing Editor Kingshuk Ghoshal
Managing Art Editor Govind Mittal

DK LONDON
Senior Editor Ashwin Khurana
Senior Art Editor Rachael Grady
Jacket Designer Surabhi Wadhwa-Gandhi
Jacket Editor Emma Dawson
Jacket Design Development Manager Sophia MTT
Producer, Pre-production Andy Hilliard
Senior Producers Jude Crozier, Mary Slater
Managing Editor Francesca Baines
Managing Art Editor Philip Letsu
Publisher Andrew Macintyre
Art Director Karen Self
Associate Publishing Director Liz Wheeler
Publishing Director Jonathan Metcalf

First published in Great Britain in 2019
by Dorling Kindersley Limited
80 Strand, London WC2R 0RL

CONTENTS

FLOWERING PLANTS 62

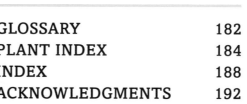

LIVING WITH PLANTS 162

Star fruit

Austrian pine

Forget-me-not

FOREWORD

Without plants, we simply wouldn't be here. These amazing organisms make the food we eat and the oxygen we breathe, using only the Sun's energy, water, and carbon dioxide from the air. We rely on plants for the grains, fruits, and vegetables that feed the world, as well as for building materials, clothing, fuel, medicines, and more. From the moment I realized their importance I became fascinated by plants, and I went on to study their secrets at university to find out more about how we rely on the 400,000 different types of plants on Earth.

From miniature mosses to colossal conifers, this book showcases the sheer diversity of plants around the world and the ways they support almost all life on Earth. The first land plants evolved around 470 million years ago and have since spread across the planet, transforming the landscape into a wide range of habitats, such as rainforests and grasslands, moorlands and swamps. Plants also changed the course of human history. Early people lived nomadic lives as hunter-gatherers until they learned how to grow crops and were able to form settled communities. This allowed populations to grow and thrive, and civilizations to develop.

Inside this book you'll discover many of the wonders of the plant world that have captured the imagination of scientists like me for centuries. You'll see the tallest trees, the

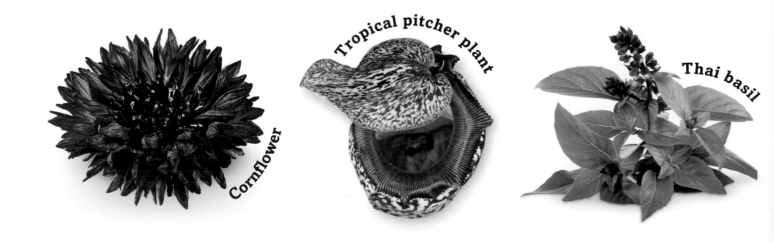
Cornflower

Tropical pitcher plant

Thai basil

Angel wings

Moulded wax plant

Dwarf pomegranate

smelliest flowers, and plants that are masters of disguise. There are plants that live for only a couple of weeks and others that live for thousands of years. You will find out how some plants use animals to pollinate their flowers and spread their seeds, and how plants defend themselves against hungry herbivores. You will even meet some plants that eat animals!

I hope this book will inspire you to take a closer look at the plants all around you, make you curious about their behaviour, and help you enjoy and wonder at these incredible and important living things.

Dr Sarah Jose

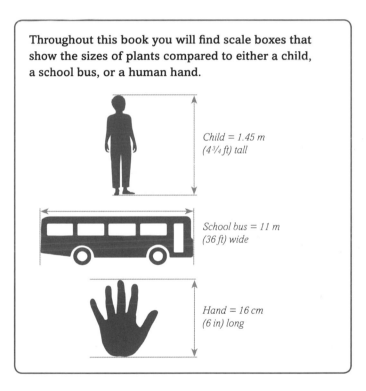

Throughout this book you will find scale boxes that show the sizes of plants compared to either a child, a school bus, or a human hand.

*Child = 1.45 m
(4¾ ft) tall*

*School bus = 11 m
(36 ft) wide*

*Hand = 16 cm
(6 in) long*

Dragon fruit

Holly

Radicchio

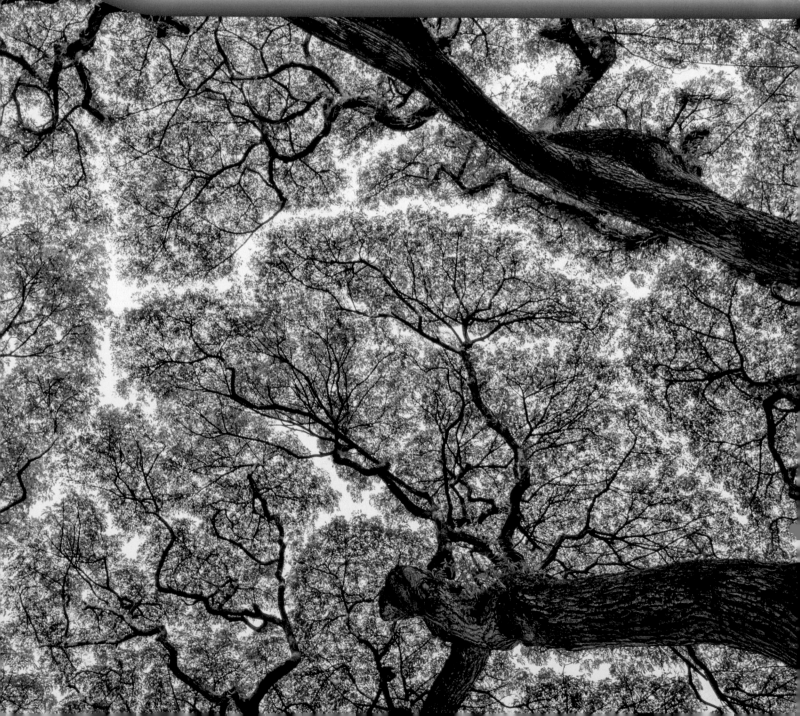

THE WORLD
OF PLANTS

Liverworts

Common liverwort

Mosses

Star moss

Hornworts

Smooth hornwort

Lycopods

Stiff clubmoss

The plant kingdom

Grasses

Little bluestem

Daisies

Figaro dahlia

There are around 400,000 different types of plant, and botanists – scientists specializing in plants – discover new ones all the time. Hundreds of millions of years ago, the first plants were small and did not flower. Over time, the process of evolution created a fantastic range of plants, from simple ferns to stunning cherry blossoms and spiky cacti. To bring order to this incredible variety, botanists divide up plants into non-flowering and flowering plants. Within these categories, there are many species, some are shown here.

PLANT KINGDOM

Flowering plants

Angiosperms, or flowering plants, make up more than 90 per cent of all plants. They produce seeds that are protected by a hard casing.

Ferns

Soft tree fern

Gymnosperms

Lodgepole pine

Angiosperms

Lupin

Monocots

Monocots have just one seed leaf, which grows into a new plant. They often have long, narrow leaves. Grasses, orchids, and palms are examples of monocots.

Dicots

Dicots have two seed leaves, which appear together when a new plant starts to grow. They mostly have broad leaves. Dicots include daisies, roses, cacti, and legumes.

Orchids

Vanda pink magic

Palms

Coconut palm

Roses

Chinese rose

Cacti

Old man of the Andes

Legumes

Snow pea

What is a plant?

Plants come in all shapes and sizes – from tiny green mosses to giant trees – but almost all plants contain a green pigment called chlorophyll. This chemical harnesses the energy of sunlight to make the food (a sugar called glucose) that the plant needs to grow. As part of this process, called photosynthesis, plants take carbon dioxide gas from the air and turn it into food, while releasing oxygen, which all animals need to breathe.

Flower > This colourful part of the plant contains the male and female cells that are responsible for producing seeds.

Tendril > This plant has a specialized stem, called a tendril, which wraps round nearby objects, helping to support the plant.

Not a plant

Lichens
A lichen is made up of algae and fungi living together. The algae help make food, while the fungi provide shade.

Corals
Corals are tiny, underwater animals with hard skeletons. To grow, they depend on algae in their tissues to make energy from sunlight.

Algae
Many algae are green, like plants, but do not have true roots, stems, and leaves. Algae can only live in water.

Fungi
Unlike plants, fungi get their food from the soil, or from other plants and animals on which they grow.

Stem > The stem supports the plant. It can be short or tall, woody or non-woody.

Leaf > This is the powerstation of a plant. Leaves use sunlight to make the energy the plant needs to grow.

Cucumber plant

Fruit > A fruit contains the plant's seeds, protecting them from harm. Colourful fruits attract animals to eat them and then spread the seeds in their droppings.

Flowering plant

This cucumber plant uses flowers to reproduce and make seeds for new plants. However, not all plants have flowers – simple plants, such as mosses and conifers, reproduce in other ways. It is sometimes difficult to tell what is a plant and what is not – seaweed and fungi, for example, are not plants.

Root > Plants use their roots to anchor themselves to the ground. Roots also draw water and nutrients from the soil to keep the plant alive.

How do roots work?

Most plants have roots, which anchor the plant in the ground. Roots soak up vital water from the soil, along with the dissolved minerals that the plant uses to grow. Grasses have tufts of fibrous roots, but most other plants grow at least one taproot, which then sprouts smaller lateral (side) roots that spread outwards.

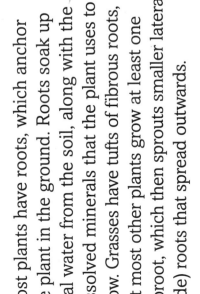

Leaf > A plant's leaves use the energy from sunlight to make sugar. Water is drawn up through the roots and sugary sap moves down from the leaves, powering the plant's growth.

Burdock root

Taproot > As a seed starts to grow, one or more strong roots push down into the soil. This is the plant's taproot and it grows only at its tip, forcing soil particles aside with a tough root cap as it grows deeper into the ground.

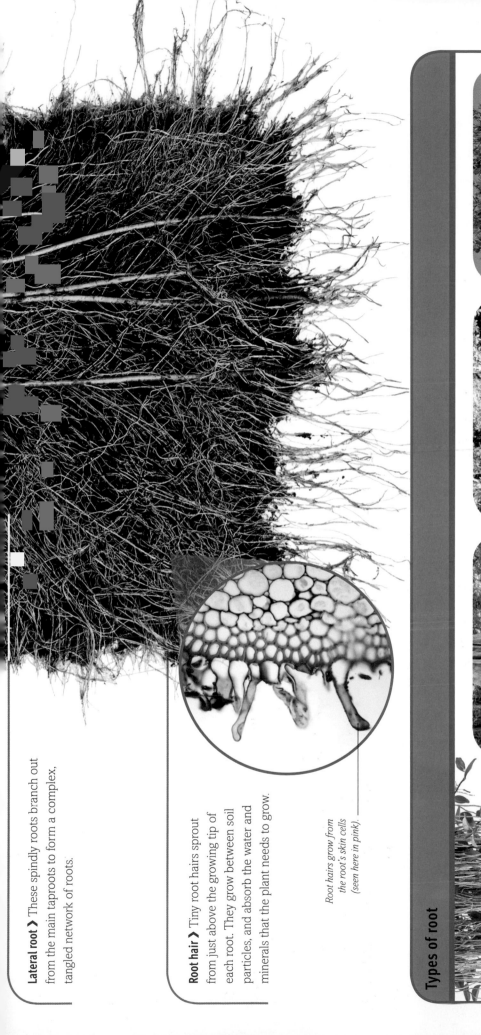

Lateral root ▶ These spindly roots branch out from the main taproots to form a complex, tangled network of roots.

Root hair ▶ Tiny root hairs sprout from just above the growing tip of each root. They grow between soil particles, and absorb the water and minerals that the plant needs to grow.

Root hairs grow from the root's skin cells (seen here in pink).

Types of root

Aerial Some plants, typically in tropical forests, grow in the treetops with roots that cling to the tree bark for support. The American pearl laceleaf grows roots that hang in the moist air to absorb essential water.

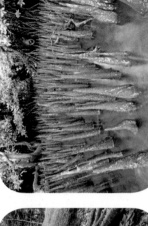

Buttress Many tropical rainforest trees are supported by roots that spread out partly above the ground. This is because most rainforest soil is not very deep and these surface roots anchor the tree in loose soil.

Pneumatophore Rooted in waterlogged, airless mud, these mangrove trees grow in swampy, subtropical, or tropical brackish (salty) water. Some have roots that grow upwards into the air to gather oxygen.

Stilt Mangroves growing on muddy tidal seashores are swept by waves at high tide. Many of these mangrove trees have stiltlike roots that arch down from their trunks to help support them in the moving water.

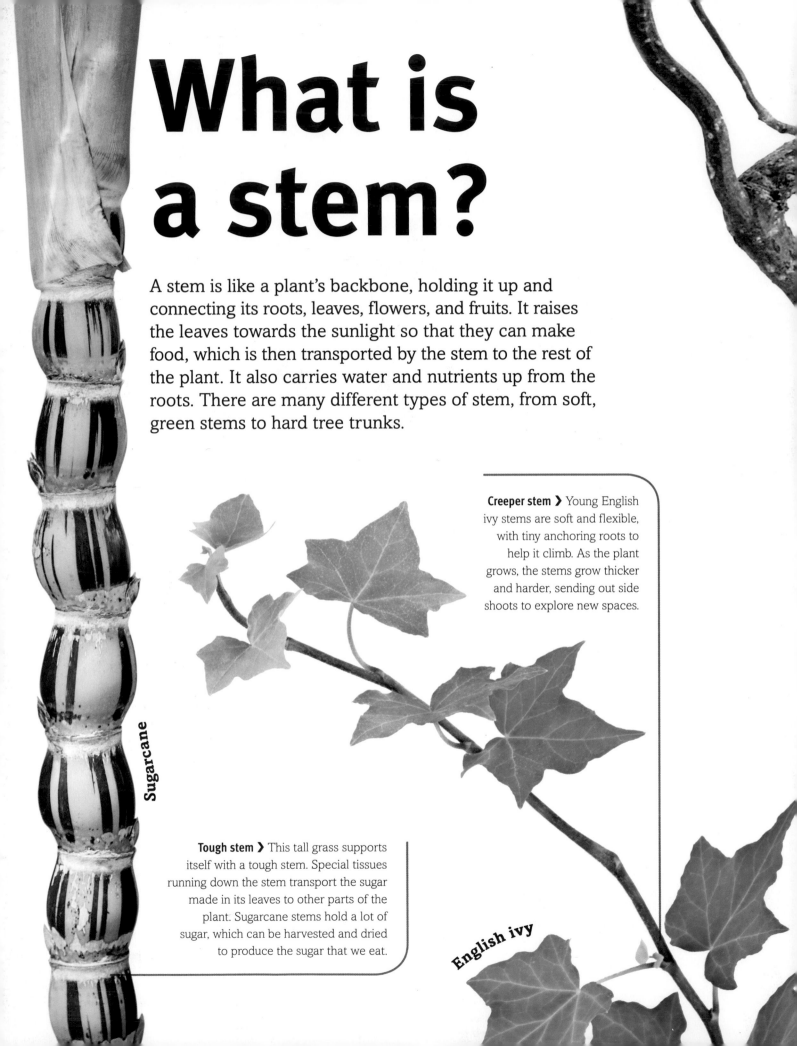

What is a stem?

A stem is like a plant's backbone, holding it up and connecting its roots, leaves, flowers, and fruits. It raises the leaves towards the sunlight so that they can make food, which is then transported by the stem to the rest of the plant. It also carries water and nutrients up from the roots. There are many different types of stem, from soft, green stems to hard tree trunks.

Creeper stem ❯ Young English ivy stems are soft and flexible, with tiny anchoring roots to help it climb. As the plant grows, the stems grow thicker and harder, sending out side shoots to explore new spaces.

Sugarcane

Tough stem ❯ This tall grass supports itself with a tough stem. Special tissues running down the stem transport the sugar made in its leaves to other parts of the plant. Sugarcane stems hold a lot of sugar, which can be harvested and dried to produce the sugar that we eat.

English ivy

Woody stem ❯ Trunks and branches are woody stems, which are stiff and strong to provide support for tall trees. They are protected by an outer covering of dead tissue bark. These stems expand by producing new layers of woody tissue each year – the growth rings that can be seen in cut tree trunks.

Corkscrew hazel

Sun rose

Soft stem ❯ The non-woody stems of many smaller plants are soft and green. They support the plant, while transporting water and nutrients.

Types of stems

There are many types of stem. Woody stems contain two layers of tissue – one transports water, and the other food in the form of sugar. In non-woody stems, these tissues are combined into tubes. Woody stems are protected by thickened bark, while non-woody stems are covered by a thin, protective tissue layer.

Tissue transporting water

Tissue transporting sugar

Soft, spongy layer

Thin outer layer

Non-woody stem

Tissue transporting sugar

Tissue transporting water

Core of woody stem

Tough, strong bark

Woody stem

Sweet sap suckers

Small bugs called aphids puncture stems to suck out the sweet, nutrient-rich liquid transported inside it. These insects do not usually kill the plant, but they can often slow down its growth, and carry diseases that might harm it.

LIVING BRIDGES
The state of Meghalaya in northeast India is one of the wettest regions in the world, with almost 12 m (39 ft) of rainfall each year. The rains flood the rivers, making travel difficult, but the local Khasi Tribe came up with a clever way to stay connected with other villages. Using the roots of the rubber fig tree, they built strong, living bridges that can hold up to 50 people at once.

This type of bridge is made by twisting the aerial roots (roots that grow above ground) of rubber fig trees around temporary bridges made of bamboo or tree trunks, which then rot away over time. Once the tree roots reach the other side of the river, they are planted into the ground so they can grow thicker and stronger. It can take about 15–20 years to build a living bridge, which can grow to more than 50 m (164 ft) in length. The strongest living bridges are more than 100 years old, with some believed to be over 500 years old. This double-decker bridge in Cherrapunji is more than 180 years old, and the local people are now adding a third level to it to attract more tourists.

How do seeds grow?

Plants are rooted to the spot, so to reproduce and spread, flowering plants make seeds from which new plants grow. A seed contains a tiny young plant called an embryo, which lies dormant (inactive) until it senses the perfect conditions to germinate and grow into a new plant.

Young shoot ❯ Next a young shoot emerges from the seed, growing upwards until it breaks out of the soil. It quickly begins to make food using sunlight.

Germination ❯ A seed lies dormant until it detects moisture and warmth. It then absorbs water from the soil, and the seed springs to life, in a process known as germination.

First root ❯ Most seeds begin germination by sending a root downwards into the soil. The root absorbs water and nutrients from the soil, and passes them on to the developing shoot.

Inside a seed

A seed is a perfectly packaged baby plant, called an embryo, protected by a hard outer coat. The embryo has a root and a shoot, and the first true leaves. It also has a food store for the embryo in "seed leaves".

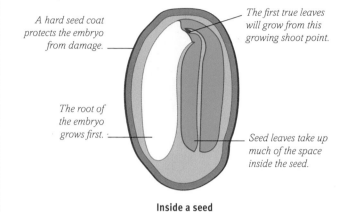

A hard seed coat protects the embryo from damage.

The first true leaves will grow from this growing shoot point.

The root of the embryo grows first.

Seed leaves take up much of the space inside the seed.

Inside a seed

Seed leaves ❯ The first leaf, or pair of leaves, in a flowering plant often looks very different to the true leaves the seedling will grow later. This is because the seed leaves were part of the embryo that lived inside the seed.

The seed case still clings to the young plant as it emerges from the ground.

New leaves will form at the top of the stem.

The root has fine hairs to help it absorb even more water.

One leaf or two?

There are two main types of flowering plants, monocots and dicots, named for the number of seed leaves they have. Monocot seeds contain one seed leaf, while dicot seeds have two.

Two broad seed leaves grow out of a dicot seed.

A single seed leaf emerges from the tip of the shoot.

Maize seed (monocot)

Germinating monocot seed

Haricot bean (dicot)

Germinating dicot seed

Early germination

Sometimes seeds germinate before they have parted from their parent plant. This early germination may take the form of shoots growing on the outside of a fruit, as seen on this strawberry. In other fruits, shoots may even burst through the fruit wall from the seeds held inside.

Germinating seed

Seed shapes

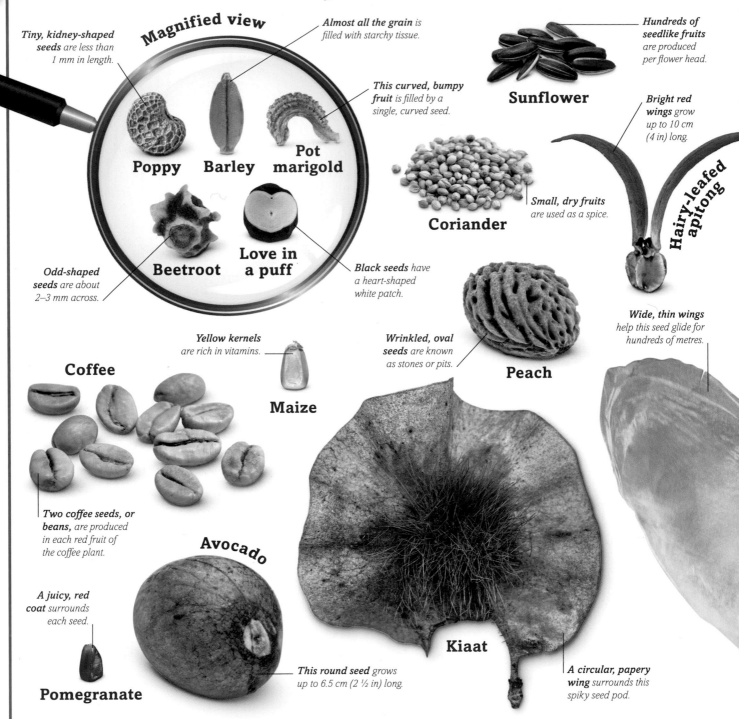

Magnified view

*Tiny, kidney-shaped **seeds** are less than 1 mm in length.*

Almost all the grain is filled with starchy tissue.

*This curved, bumpy **fruit** is filled by a single, curved seed.*

Poppy

Barley

Pot marigold

*Odd-shaped **seeds** are about 2–3 mm across.*

Beetroot

Love in a puff

Black seeds have a heart-shaped white patch.

Hundreds of seedlike fruits are produced per flower head.

Sunflower

*Bright red **wings** grow up to 10 cm (4 in) long.*

Coriander

Small, dry fruits are used as a spice.

Hairy-leafed apitong

Wide, thin wings help this seed glide for hundreds of metres.

*Wrinkled, oval **seeds** are known as stones or pits.*

Peach

Yellow kernels are rich in vitamins.

Coffee

Maize

*Two coffee seeds, or **beans**, are produced in each red fruit of the coffee plant.*

Avocado

*A juicy, red **coat** surrounds each seed.*

Pomegranate

This round seed grows up to 6.5 cm (2 ½ in) long.

Kiaat

*A circular, papery **wing** surrounds this spiky seed pod.*

A seed is a small package that protects a young plant and contains all the nutrients the plant will need to germinate. Although all seeds do the same job, they come in a wide range of shapes and sizes, to help each one to survive in its particular environment and spread without being eaten by hungry animals.

The giant **coco de mer** seed is able to hold a lot of nutrients so that the new plant has enough energy to grow out of its mother's shadow. The **poppy** has another survival strategy – rather than one big seed, it produces tens of thousands of tiny seeds to maximize its chances. The spiky coats of the **horse chestnut** seed and the **kiaat** seed pod

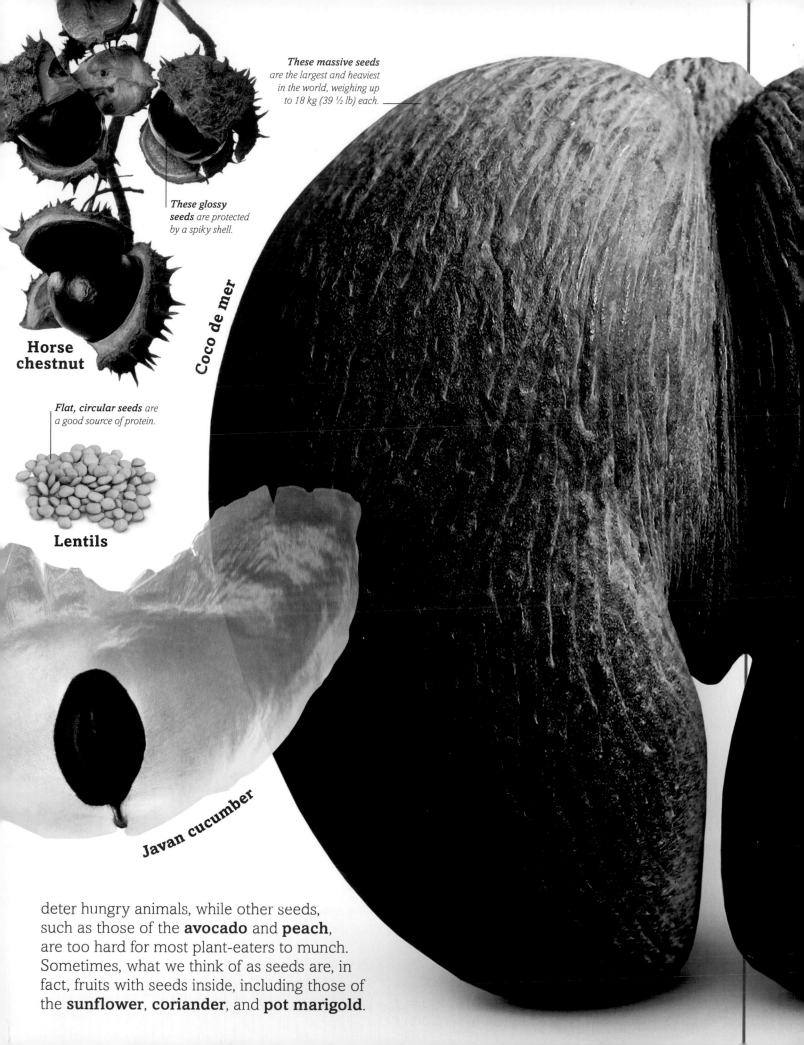

These massive seeds are the largest and heaviest in the world, weighing up to 18 kg (39 ½ lb) each.

These glossy **seeds** *are protected by a spiky shell.*

Horse chestnut

Coco de mer

Flat, circular seeds are a good source of protein.

Lentils

Javan cucumber

deter hungry animals, while other seeds, such as those of the **avocado** and **peach**, are too hard for most plant-eaters to munch. Sometimes, what we think of as seeds are, in fact, fruits with seeds inside, including those of the **sunflower**, **coriander**, and **pot marigold**.

Blackberry

Juicy berries are eaten by harvest mice, which pass the seeds in their droppings.

Dandelion

Scattering seeds

When shaken, lotus seeds fall from the dried seed pod and into the lake or pond in which the plant grows.

Lotus

Burdock seeds form spiky heads that can can grow up to 3 cm (1 in) across.

Burdock

Between 90 and 110 feathery bristles radiate outwards to form a parachute on every seed.

Plants are anchored by roots and can't move from one place to another. If they dropped their seeds where they stood, the new plants would be in competition for nutrients and sunlight. So plants have developed many ways to make sure their seeds scatter far and wide to take advantage of new places in which to grow. They use exploding seed pods, animals, the wind, or even water to spread their seeds.

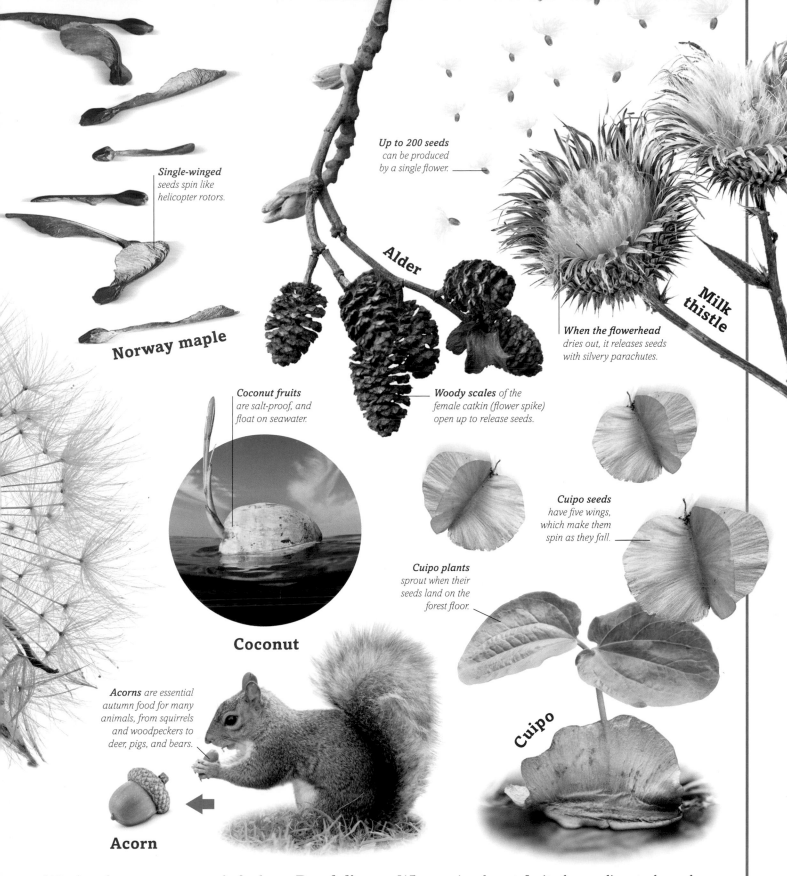

Single-winged seeds spin like helicopter rotors.

Norway maple

Up to 200 seeds can be produced by a single flower.

Alder

When the flowerhead dries out, it releases seeds with silvery parachutes.

Milk thistle

Coconut fruits are salt-proof, and float on seawater.

Woody scales of the female catkin (flower spike) open up to release seeds.

Cuipo seeds have five wings, which make them spin as they fall.

Cuipo plants sprout when their seeds land on the forest floor.

Coconut

Acorns are essential autumn food for many animals, from squirrels and woodpeckers to deer, pigs, and bears.

Cuipo

Acorn

Wind and water carry seeds furthest. **Dandelion** and **milk thistle** seeds have parachutes that carry them on the breeze, while **maple** and **cuipo** seeds spin as they catch the wind and fall from the tree canopy. **Coconut** seeds can travel hundreds of kilometres on ocean currents. Animals are also important seed-spreaders.

When animals eat fruit, the undigested seeds inside the fruit are passed out in their droppings. **Burdock** seeds are covered in hooks that get caught in animal fur and transported. Squirrels bury hundreds of **acorns** each autumn, to eat in winter. The ones they forget about germinate into new oak trees.

Spreading without seeds

Mint

Tiny plantlets with roots form along the fleshy leaves.

Plantlet

Underground stems can send out new shoots around the mother plant.

Iris

Spreading underground stems are partially visible through a thin layer of soil.

Stems grow from the base of the old tree.

Beech

Mother of thousands

Each leaf can produce dozens of tiny plantlets.

Some plants have evolved ways to spread quickly over an area without seeds. To do this they make perfect copies of themselves using modified stems, forming underground storage organs, or growing baby plants on the margins of their leaves.

Plants such as **mint**, **strawberry**, and **bamboo** send out long stems, either just below or on top of the soil, which can put down roots and grow into whole new plants. The creeping underground stems, or rhizomes, of some **irises** also send up new plants as they spread. Other plants, such as **sweet potatoes**, produce underground storage

Spider plant

These stems grow roots and then leaves to become independent plants.

Parent plant sends out horizontal stems along the soil.

New bamboo shoots can grow up to 90 cm (35 in) in a day.

Strawberry

Plantlets grow on dangling stems.

STEM RUNNERS

The strawberry plant produces long stems called runners that run along or just under the soil. New strawberry plants grow at the knots, or nodes, on the runners, quickly colonizing an area with good soil.

Runners lay down roots before new plants can grow.

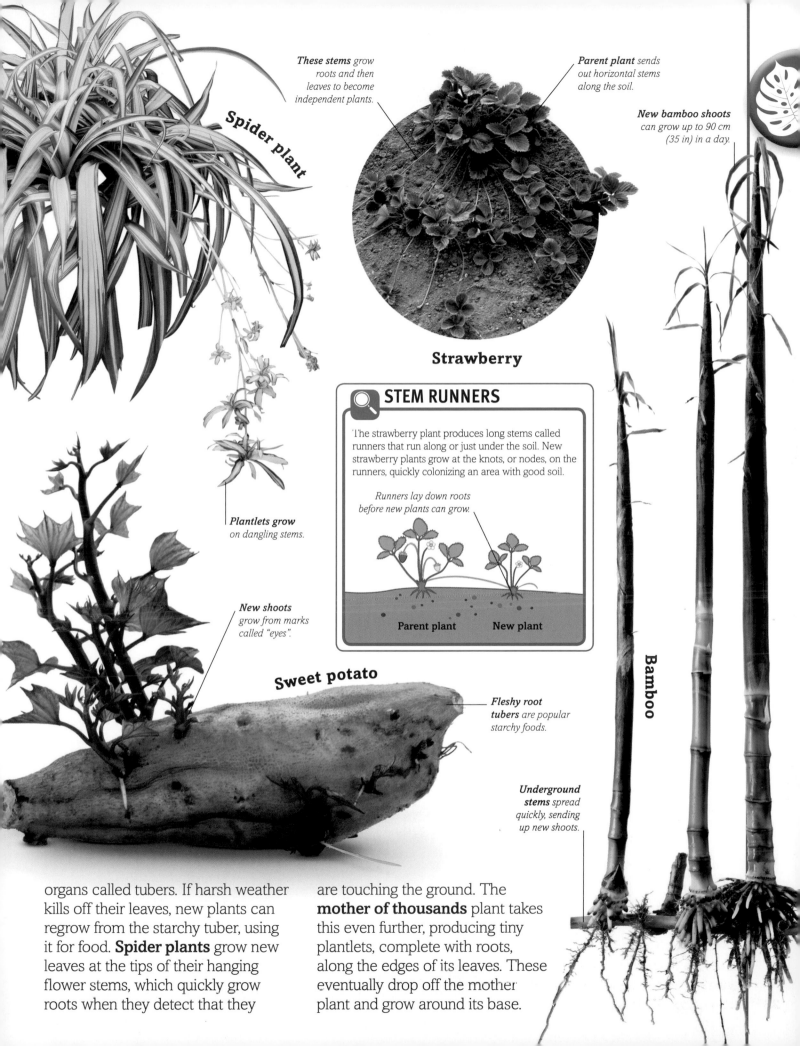

Parent plant   New plant

New shoots grow from marks called "eyes".

Sweet potato

Fleshy root tubers are popular starchy foods.

Bamboo

Underground stems spread quickly, sending up new shoots.

organs called tubers. If harsh weather kills off their leaves, new plants can regrow from the starchy tuber, using it for food. **Spider plants** grow new leaves at the tips of their hanging flower stems, which quickly grow roots when they detect that they are touching the ground. The **mother of thousands** plant takes this even further, producing tiny plantlets, complete with roots, along the edges of its leaves. These eventually drop off the mother plant and grow around its base.

The life cycle of a plant

Flowering plants may have a lifespan of just months, or many years. A poppy will germinate, flower, set seed, and die within a year, and is known as an annual plant. Other flowering plants live for several years, building up the food reserves they need and storing it. These are called perennial plants. The harsher the climate, the longer it can take for a plant to complete its life cycle.

8 ▲ The fruit develops and ripens. New seeds are dispersed by the wind and the cycle starts again.

1 ▲ Seeds lie dormant (inactive) waiting for the right conditions to germinate.

2 ◀ Germination begins when there is enough water, warmth, and light for the seeds to sprout their first root and then a shoot.

Late bloomer

High in the cold Andes Mountains of South America, the queen of the Andes plant grows very slowly. It takes more than 80 years to bloom and grows a massive flower spike nearly 10 m (30 ft) tall, with up to 30,000 flowers, dwarfing the surrounding plants. After shedding millions of seeds, it dies.

3 ▲ Seedlings begin to produce leaves to gather light, and more roots to absorb water from the soil to help them grow.

4 ▶ Flower buds develop. In plants that flower every year (annuals) such as poppies, the bud can form within a few weeks of germination.

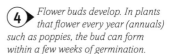

Poppy

7 As soon as a flower is pollinated, it sheds its petals. Seeds form inside the fruit.

5 Protected within the green sepals (leaf-shaped, and sometimes hairy structures at the base of a flower), the bud grows colourful petals. When the flower is ready to open, the petals burst out.

6 Once the petals open up, insects, such as bees, are attracted to the sweet nectar inside and pollinate the flower.

What is a leaf?

Leaves are usually flat, green structures that grow from plant stems. Although they come in many shapes and sizes, almost all of them capture sunlight and produce food for the plant. Leaves get their green colour from a pigment called chlorophyll, which uses sunlight to produce food in a process called photosynthesis.

Small netted veins > Networks of tiny veins connect the green tissues of the leaf to the main vein inside the midrib, and the stem beyond.

Stomata > Tiny pores on the underside of the leaf, called stomata, open during the day to take in carbon dioxide, but close at night to avoid losing too much water.

Underside of apple leaf

Petiole > This is the stiff stalk connecting the leaf to the plant stem. In some plants, these stalks can help leaves move and follow the Sun in order to absorb more light.

Blade > The flat part of the leaf is called the leaf blade. It is the green tissue that absorbs sunlight to make the sugar the plant needs to grow.

Midrib ❯ Running along the centre of the leaf, this thickened area contains the central vein. It also provides support to the leaf to prevent it from bending and breaking.

Apple leaf

Vein ❯ Plant veins have two types of tube running through them. One type, called xylem, carries water from the roots to the shoots. The other type, known as phloem, transports sugars around the plant.

Photosynthesis

Plants make their own food in a process called photosynthesis. Their leaves contain a light-harvesting pigment called chlorophyll. This green chemical uses the Sun's energy to convert carbon dioxide from the air and water from the soil into food (in the form of sugars) and oxygen.

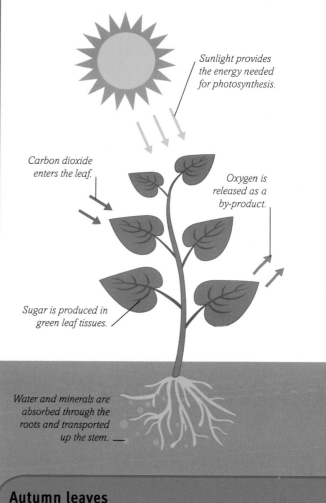

Sunlight provides the energy needed for photosynthesis.

Carbon dioxide enters the leaf.

Oxygen is released as a by-product.

Sugar is produced in green leaf tissues.

Water and minerals are absorbed through the roots and transported up the stem.

Autumn leaves

As autumn approaches, the green pigment chlorophyll is replaced at a slower rate than it is used up. The reduced chlorophyll levels mean other leaf pigments, including orange-yellow ones, become more obvious. At the same time, plants start producing red-purple pigments. These changes result in the beautiful autumnal displays of leaf colour.

Maple leaves in autumn

Simple leaves

Young leaves have five sharp points, while older leaves are rounder.

Spear-shaped

English ivy

Dandelion

These jagged leaves contain a bitter milky sap called latex.

Divided

Leaves develop large holes as the plant ages, and can grow up to 90 cm (35 in) long.

Swiss-cheese plant

Amazonian water lily

Sugar maple leaves turn red before falling in the autumn.

Palm-shaped

Circular

Sugar maple

Heart-shaped

Veins grow from the stalk at the centre of the leaf.

Oval-shaped

Nasturtium   Circular

Spiky edges protect the leaves from grazing animals.

Holly

A leaf typically consists of a flat surface called a blade, which carries a network of veins. These veins support the leaves and transport the water and minerals to them from the rest of the plant. A simple leaf has a single, undivided blade.

Simple leaves come in many shapes and sizes, and those best suited to their habitat are the most likely to thrive. In wet, rainforest conditions, plants have big leaves, while plants in drier locations usually have small leaves. Some plants, such as **English ivy** and **ginkgo**, change their leaf shape

Ginkgo

Fan-shaped

Veins branch out like a fan instead of forming a network.

These giant leaves grow up to 3 m (9¾ ft) across.

Arrow-shaped

Oak

Oak leaves, which can grow up to 10 cm (4 in) long, turn brown and fall off in the autumn.

Eucalyptus

Divided

Jagged edges are more common in leaves from colder countries.

Waxy leaves repel water, so rainwater flows quickly off this rainforest plant.

Birch

Triangular

This leaf contains a toxic oil to avoid being eaten by predators.

Lance-shaped

Elephant's ear

Thin, bladelike leaves are common in grass plants.

Linear

Wheat

as they grow and get more access to sunlight. The **Swiss-cheese plant** and **elephant's ear** grow in rainforests, so have waxy, pointy leaves to help rainwater run off. Another rainforest plant, the **Amazonian water lily**, has giant leaves that spread across lakes to capture as much sunlight as possible. Although the reasons remain unclear, scientists believe the jagged leaf edges of **sugar maple** and **birch** may help keep them slightly warmer than smooth edges would, allowing the plants to grow faster in cool spring weather.

Compound leaves

Sensitive plant

Leaflets fold shut in about three seconds if touched.

Divided twice

Feathery leaves turn a golden yellow in the autumn.

Stinking toe

Two leaflets

Shiny green leaflets look like a cow's toes, but this plant gets its name from its stinky fruit.

Tamarind

Lupin

Rounded lupin leaves have up to 17 leaflets.

Multiple leaflets

Arranged like a **closed fan** when young, the lupin's leaves **unfold** as it grows.

Divided into an even number of leaflets

Oval leaflets fold up at night and open during the day.

A compound leaf is one that is divided into two or more parts called leaflets. These leaflets either grow along the stalk like a feather, or from a single point like a fan. Compound leaves come in a wide range of shapes and sizes.

A compound leaf has separate leaflets with less individual surface area than a simple leaf. In a dry region, this helps the plant to reduce the amount of water lost through evaporation. Compound leaves, like that of the **lupin**, flutter less in windy conditions than simple leaves,

Honey locust

Veins from the main leaf stalk run through each leaflet.

Divided into an odd number of leaflets

Four heart-shaped leaflets grow from a single stalk.

Five leaflets

Horse chestnut

Four leaflets

Four-leaved pink sorrel

Flat leaf stalk looks like a second leaf below the true leaf.

Leaf stalk (bottom) looks like true leaf

Pomelo

Silver fern

Silvery undersides of the leaves give this fern its name.

Divided twice

A whitish, V-shaped band is typical in white clover leaflets.

White clover

Three leaflets

LONGEST LEAF

Raffia palm leaves grow a whopping 25 m (82 ft) long – more than twice as long as a school bus.

25 m (82 ft) long

Raffia palm leaf

making them less likely to break off. Having compound leaves can also help the plants avoid being eaten. Leaflets of the **sensitive plant** quickly fold up if touched by hungry animals, while **tamarind** leaflets close up at night to appear smaller and less tasty to plant-eaters.

Some compound leaves grow very quickly, which helps trees, such as the **honey locust**, harness as much sunlight as possible before losing their leaves in winter. The **pomelo** has a rare type of compound leaf with a flat stalk that looks like a second leaf, which also helps capture sunlight.

Plants with patterns

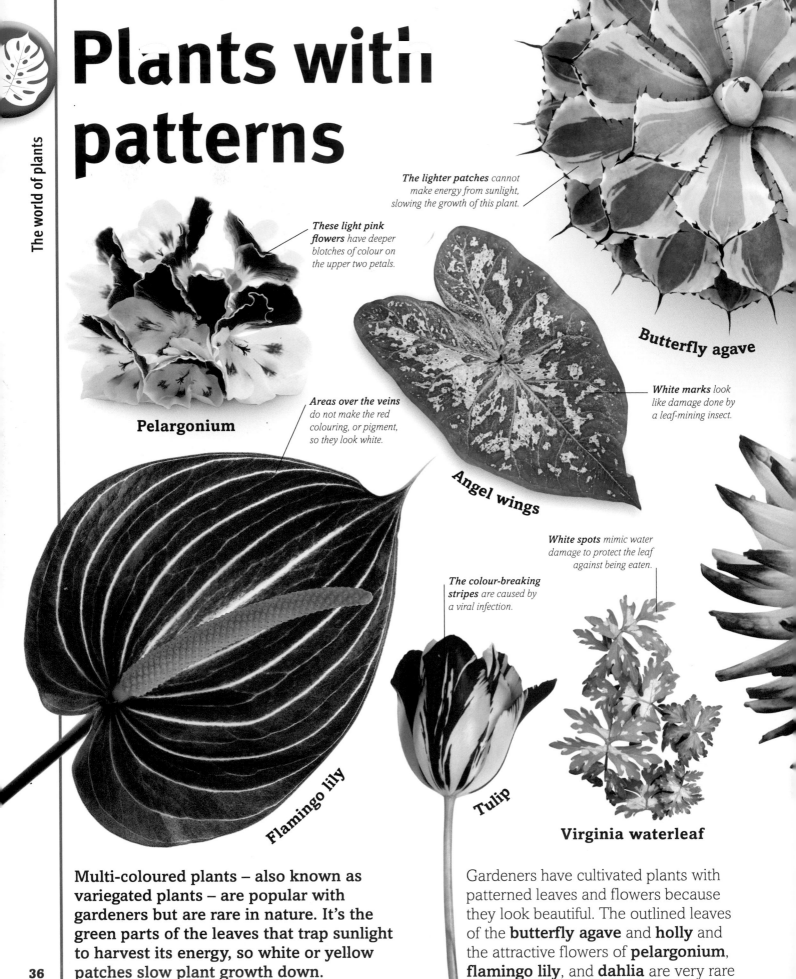

The lighter patches cannot make energy from sunlight, slowing the growth of this plant.

These light pink flowers have deeper blotches of colour on the upper two petals.

Pelargonium

Butterfly agave

White marks look like damage done by a leaf-mining insect.

Angel wings

Areas over the veins do not make the red colouring, or pigment, so they look white.

White spots mimic water damage to protect the leaf against being eaten.

The colour-breaking stripes are caused by a viral infection.

Flamingo lily

Tulip

Virginia waterleaf

Multi-coloured plants – also known as variegated plants – are popular with gardeners but are rare in nature. It's the green parts of the leaves that trap sunlight to harvest its energy, so white or yellow patches slow plant growth down.

Gardeners have cultivated plants with patterned leaves and flowers because they look beautiful. The outlined leaves of the **butterfly agave** and **holly** and the attractive flowers of **pelargonium**, **flamingo lily**, and **dahlia** are very rare

Begonia

Rose

White patches do not have the ability to make colour.

Calathea

The silvery patches can produce food too, helping this plant to grow.

Begonias produce **seeds** so **small** they look like **dust**.

These spiky leaves are very hardy. The holly plant can grow up to 15 m (50 ft) in height.

Holly

Calathea leaves come in many patterns, from mosaic to striped.

Purple-blue flowers are marked with white spots of different sizes and resemble a starry night sky.

Dahlia

Only the tips of this flower make the pink pigment.

Petunia

in wild plants. In the 17th century, striped **tulip** flowers were very fashionable in the Netherlands and sold for huge amounts of money. It was later found that the delicate markings on the tulips were actually the result of a viral infection. **Angel wings** and

Virginia waterleaf are among the few plants that have naturally patterned leaves. Both have white spots on their leaves, which make them appear damaged and less appetizing. This greatly reduces the chance of insects eating their leaves.

SYMMETRICAL SWIRLS

Twirl a sunflower around in your fingers and the pattern at the centre of the flower head looks the same from every side. This is because the sunflower head is radially symmetrical – the florets form two sets of spirals starting at the same point somewhere in the centre of the flower, before turning in opposite directions, one clockwise and the other anti-clockwise.

Radial symmetry appears throughout the plant world, from daisies to pine cones. The spirals follow a pattern known as the Fibonacci sequence, named after the Italian mathematician who discovered it. In this sequence, each number is the sum of the previous two. The pattern starts 1, 1, 2, 3, 5, 8, 13, 21, and so on. The reason why Fibonacci numbers are common in nature is because this is the best way to pack the most flowers, leaves, or seeds into a tight space. A sunflower head is made up of many tiny florets – the dark rods in the picture are opened florets, while those in the centre are unopen ones. Each new floret grows at an angle to the previous one, leaving no gaps and maximizing its exposure to pollinators.

Self defence

Animals can run from their predators, but plants have no way of escaping hungry plant-eaters. Instead, they have developed some clever ways of making themselves look and taste as unappealing or dangerous as possible, encouraging animals to look elsewhere for a meal. Plant defences range from spiky thorns to toxic chemicals.

Needlelike crystals line the blue agave's leaves, making them an unpleasant mouthful.

Silver-grey crystals

Spiky leaf edges protect these succulent leaves.

Blue agave

Camel thorn

Fully developed thorns may grow up to 6 cm (2 ¼ in) long.

Tea leaves contain tannin, a bitter-tasting chemical that deters animals from eating them.

Spines on the stem protect the plant from hungry animals.

Tea

Thistle

These woolly leaves are difficult for insects to munch.

These swollen parts provide hollow homes for ants that help ward off predators, so protecting the plant.

Ant fern

Lamb's ear

To deter predators, some plants, including the **camel thorn**, produce sharp branches called thorns, while others, such as **gorse**, make sharp leaves known as spines. Prickles are extensions of the stems of plants such as **roses**. Another plant defence strategy is the use of chemicals. Plants, such as **tea**, **common milkweed**, and **blue agave**, produce nasty tasting or irritating chemicals to put off any animal that takes a bite. The spots on **passion flower** leaves are a clever defence called mimicry – the plant's leaves pretend to be infested by butterfly eggs, which deters real butterflies looking for a "healthy" leaf.

Passion flower

Leaf spots resemble yellow butterfly eggs.

Thorns grow up to 7 cm (3 in) long.

Common milkweed

The gummy white sap of this flowering plant is toxic to many plant-eating mammals.

Whistling thorn acacia

Ants live inside these swollen thorns, protecting the plant from herbivores.

The stiff spines that cover the plant can be up to 6.5 cm (2 ½ in) long.

Small birds **nest in spiky gorse** bushes to protect themselves from predators.

Gorse

Buds contain yellow flowers with a coconut scent.

Stems and leaves are covered in tiny stinging hairs.

Stinging nettle

Needlelike hairs can inject a painful mix of chemicals.

Stinging hairs

Rose

Downward-pointing prickles grow on the stems of roses to deter predators from climbing up.

Plants and nitrogen

Plants use the energy of sunlight to turn carbon dioxide and water into the sugars they need to help them grow. To do this, they also need proteins that contain nitrogen. Although this vital gas makes up two-thirds of the air we breathe, plants cannot absorb nitrogen from the air. Instead, they rely on tiny organisms in the soil to make nitrates both from the nitrogen in the air, and from the decaying remains of living things.

Nitrogen cycle

All plants, animals, and other living things contain nitrogen. When they die, their remains are broken down by fungi and bacteria. This eventually forms nitrates, which plants can use to make proteins that can be eaten by animals. Nitrogen is recycled continuously between the air, soil, and living things in this way – a process called the nitrogen cycle.

1 Nitrogen gas enters the soil from the air. Lightning can also change nitrogen gas into nitrates.

2 Some bacteria in the soil can change nitrogen gas into ammonia, which can be turned into nitrates. Similar bacteria, called nitrogen-fixing bacteria, live in the roots of plants such as peas.

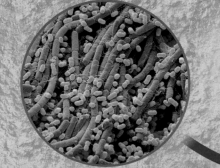

3 Plants absorb nitrates dissolved in the water that their roots soak up from the soil. They use the nitrates to make the proteins essential for growth.

Nitrogen-fixing bacteria

Nitrogen deficiency

If a plant is short of nitrogen, it cannot make enough protein and does not grow properly. It also cannot make enough of the chlorophyll that makes its leaves green, and the edges of its leaves turn pale or even yellow.

Nitrogen-deficient grape leaf

4 *Animals, such as cows, eat plants. They digest the plant proteins to make the animal proteins their bodies need.*

5 *Animal waste, such as dung and urine, returns nitrogen-containing compounds that can be turned into nitrates to the soil.*

7 *Some kinds of bacteria in the soil turn nitrates back into nitrogen gas, which is released into the air.*

6 *Some fungi and bacteria living in the soil feed on animal waste, or on the decaying remains of dead animals and plants. They break down nitrogen-containing compounds to release nitrates into the soil.*

Decomposing fungi

NON-FLOWERING PLANTS

Non-flowering plants

The most ancient land plants on Earth are the non-flowering plants that evolved hundreds of millions of years ago. The earliest were simple plants such as liverworts, mosses, and hornworts, which grow in damp places to avoid drying out. Ferns are more complex but still have to live in moist environments. Instead of producing seeds, almost all non-flowering plants reproduce using tiny spores, which are carried away by wind or water. Only the gymnosperms, a group of non-flowering plants that includes conifers, produce seed-bearing cones instead.

Moss life cycle

A moss's spore capsule releases spores into the wind. When they land these spores grow into leafy shoots with tiny sex organs. When it rains, male sperm cells are able to reach eggs and fertilize them. Each fertilized egg grows a new shoot, and the cycle continues.

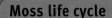

Spore capsule

Male *Female*

1. Scattering spores **2. Sex organs develop**

Raindrops allow male sperm cells to swim over to the eggs.

Spore-producing shoot

4. Spore capsule grows **3. Fertilization**

Food factory ❯ The green leaflike part of this moss, called the gametophyte, produces food using energy from sunlight. It does not contain veins to transport water and nutrients but its surface is so thin that these simply soak through.

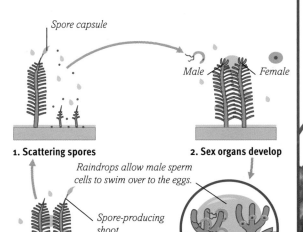

Capsule ❯ A spore-producing capsule forms at the tip of each threadlike sporophyte. When the spores are mature, the lid of the capsule breaks off to reveal an opening, through which the spores are released. Every capsule contains hundreds of thousands of tiny spores, which are carried off on the wind.

Brown sporophytes do not make their own food, relying on the green gametophyte instead.

Capillary thread moss

Liverwort
The first land plants were the tiny liverworts, which appeared around 470 million years ago. Around 9,000 liverwort species exist today.

Moss
Mosses grow in fluffy clumps, often in shady areas. Although they may look similar, 12,000 different types of moss exist around the world.

Hornwort
These humidity-loving plants, which are named for their horn-shaped sporophytes, can even grow underwater.

Club moss
The spore-producing brown spikes of club mosses are held on mosslike stems, but unlike mosses, the green parts are the sporophytes.

Horsetails
Horsetails have thin, hairlike leaves that run up their stems like a bottlebrush, and produce spores in conelike structures at the stem tip.

Sporophyte ❯ The spore-producing, columnlike structure rising from the green body of the moss is a sporophyte. It starts to grow when a female egg cell is fertilized by a male sperm cell.

Ancient plants

The first animals lived in a world filled with plants, but this vegetation looked different to what we see around us today. The earliest dinosaurs would not have seen flowers, and the plant-eaters would have chewed mosses and horsetails instead of grasses. Many of these ancient plants have disappeared, but some continue to thrive today.

Common tamarisk moss

These feathery shoots look like tiny fern fronds.

Forest star moss

Twisted moss

Star-shaped shoots range from a yellow-green to a reddish brown colour.

Spore-producing stems grow upright, allowing the spores to fly over a greater distance.

Marsh clubmoss

Mosses absorb water and nutrients from rain and dust.

This tiny, leafy liverwort grows on damp soil.

Common kettlewort

Glossy shoots give this plant its name.

Glittering wood moss

The first land plants appeared around the same time as the first insects. The earliest liverworts, relatives of the **common kettlewort** and **common liverwort**, evolved about 470 million years ago. They did not have roots, stems, or flowers but lived in damp places and simply absorbed water through their surface. Later came hornworts and mosses, many of which had more complex, leaflike shoots, like those of the modern **tamarisk moss** and the **glittering wood moss**. Without veins to carry water and nutrients from the soil to the shoots, these plants remain small. However, club mosses and horsetails, such as the **marsh clubmoss**, **fir clubmoss**, and **meadow horsetail**, have veins running up their stems, and so grow taller.

Spongelike moss can store huge amounts of water.

Common haircap

This unusually tall moss can grow up to 40 cm (15¾ in).

Sphagnum

🔍 HEALING MOSS

Sphagnum moss is absorbent and very acidic, so it prevents the growth of bacteria and fungi. During World War I (1914–1918), bandages were sometimes wrapped around sphagnum moss and used as dressings for soldiers. This stopped their wounds from becoming infected and helped them heal faster.

Dressing made of sphagnum moss

Sphagnum bandage roll

Scientists **study** the common liverwort to learn how **plants evolved**.

These tiny upright stems look like little conifers.

The young plants growing inside these cups are splashed out by raindrops.

Common liverwort

Meadow horsetail

Cuplike structure

Spore-producing cones grow at the tips of fertile stems.

Each capsule produces thousands of tiny spores.

Velvet feather-moss

Fir clubmoss

Frond ❯ Fern leaves are called fronds. These are usually divided into smaller sections, which increases the leaf's surface area so it can capture more sunlight. Fronds not only carry out photosynthesis, using the energy from sunlight to make food for the fern, they are also important for reproduction.

Wood fern

Pinna ❯ Each small segment of a fern frond growing from the central stalk, or rachis, is called a pinna.

What is a fern?

Fiddlehead ❯ New fronds develop as tightly curled spirals called fiddleheads, which unfurl as the leaf grows.

Ferns are non-flowering plants that do not produce seeds. Instead, they reproduce using tiny spores, which are carried on the wind. Fern leaves are known as fronds, and they grow from underground stems. Spores are made on the underside of fronds.

Root ❯ The roots of ferns are very similar to those of flowering plants. They absorb water and nutrients from the soil, and help to anchor the fern into the ground.

Sori ❯ Spores are produced in brown structures called sori on the underside of the fronds. These sori can be arranged in speckles or lines, depending on the type of fern.

Rachis ❯ The top part of the stalk is known as the rachis. It is the backbone of the frond.

Stipe ❯ The stiff stem at the bottom of the plant is known as the stipe. It is often covered with scales or hairs, for protection.

Rhizome ❯ The main stem of most ferns is known as the rhizome. It sits either on the soil's surface or just below, although in some tree ferns the stems can develop into a tall woody trunk. The fronds of the fern emerge from the rhizome, which is often too short to be seen.

Fossil fern

Ferns first appeared almost 360 million years ago, among mossy swamps. Some large, treelike ferns had fronds as long as 3 m (9 ¾ ft). The fossil below shows an extinct fern that looks very similar to modern ferns, such as the wood fern.

The comblike arrangement of leaflets earns this fern its name Pecopteris – *the Greek word for comb.*

***Pecopteris* fern fossil**

51

Fern fronds

Wood fern

This feather-shaped fern is native to much of Europe, Asia, and North America.

These simple fronds are said to look like deer tongues.

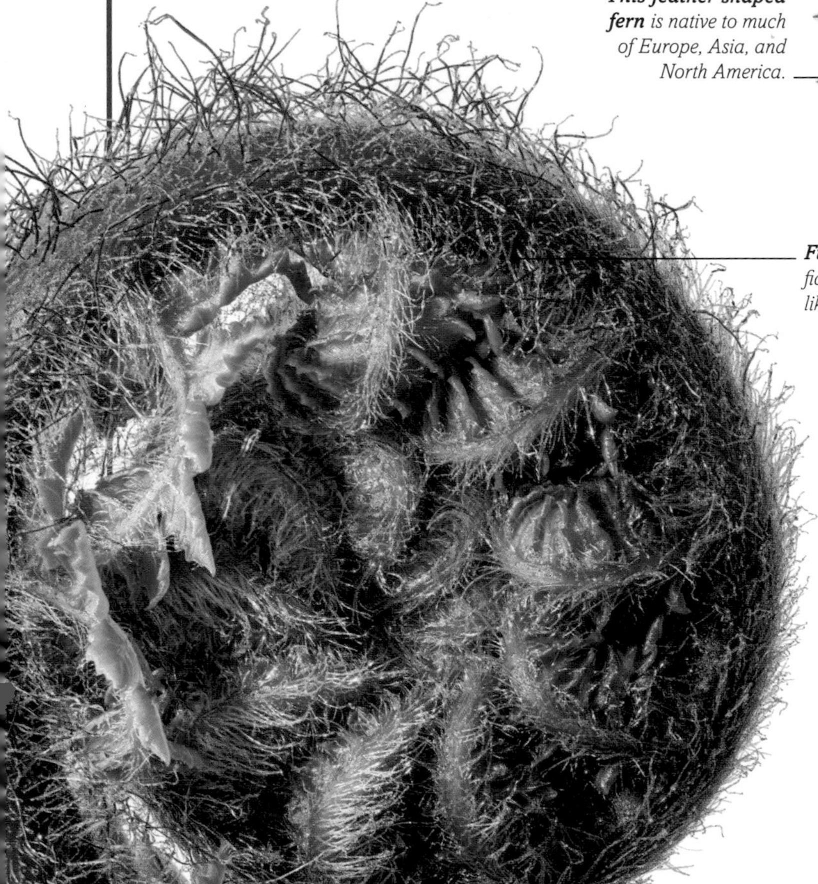

Furled fronds are known as fiddleheads because they look like the scrolls of violins.

Hart's tongue fern

Clumps of fronds grow from a short stem at the base.

Soft shield fern

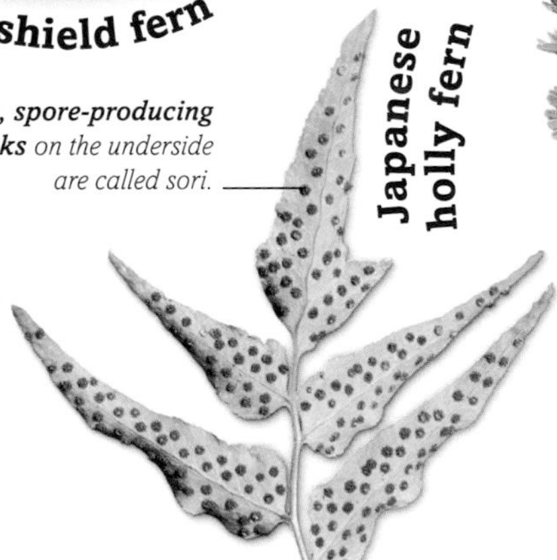

Soft tree fern

Treelike habit

Brown, spore-producing specks on the underside are called sori.

Japanese holly fern

Ferns are among the most primitive land plants. As most live on shady forest floors, they make large leaves, called fronds, to help them gather as much sunlight as possible. Many ferns share a distinctive leaf shape, with leaflets that divide, and then divide again. Ferns do not produce flowers. Instead, they grow tiny spores on the underside of their leaves, which are then blown by the wind and eventually grow into new plants.

Common maidenhair fern

Several fan-shaped leaflets form each frond.

Heart leaf fern

These glossy leaves can be heart- or arrow-shaped.

The leaves of this fern are silvery in spring and green in summer.

Ant fern

Japanese painted fern

Fossil records show that **ferns** date back **360 million years**.

Ostrich fern

The tall clumping leaves can unfurl to 170 cm (67 in) long.

Carrot fern

The feathery fronds of this plant resemble carrot leaves.

Spore-producing cups line the edges of each frond.

Leaf segments unfurl as the main stalk unrolls.

Bracken

Tufts of bracken thrive in open forests and pastures.

Bracken on forest floor

There are about 10,500 known species of fern, some of which have simple undivided fronds, such as those of the **hart's tongue fern** and the **heart leaf fern**. Most are green, but a few have unusual colours, like the purple-veined, silvery leaves of the **Japanese painted fern**. In many species, the spore-producing brown regions on the underside of fronds are arranged in distinct patterns or shapes, such as the lines of speckles on the **Japanese holly fern**. The tiny spores are usually carried away by the wind, although ants living in the hollow stems of the **ant fern** may also help this plant to spread its spores.

DINOSAUR DIET
Until about 140 million years ago, there were no flowering plants anywhere on Earth. Some gigantic plant-eating dinosaurs of the Jurassic period browsed in the treetops for the tough, fibrous foliage of pine trees that existed at the time. Others reached down to pluck the fronds of low-growing and nutritious ferns and horsetails.

During this time, the climate was warm and moist almost everywhere, with no polar ice. This encouraged the growth of dense forests of conifers, ginkgos, club mosses, cycads, and tree ferns that covered much of the land. Dinosaurs such as these two *Diplodocus*, which lived in what is now North America, had long, flexible necks for stretching high into the trees to feed. They could even rear up on their hind legs for extra height. Similar to modern elephants, they also would have broken down a lot of trees, creating open areas where smaller plants such as ferns could flourish. *Diplodocus* fed on these too, combing the stems through their peglike teeth to strip away the green foliage, and gulping it down without chewing.

What is a conifer cone?

A conifer cone contains the male or female cells of conifer trees. In non-flowering plants such as pine trees, cones are the equivalent of a flower. The seeds of conifers are not contained in fruits, but develop between the scales of the pollinated female cones. The scales protect the seeds until they are fully developed, then open up to release their seeds.

Closed cone scales ❯ The female cones contain ovules (clusters of female cells) that will develop into seeds if they are fertilized by pollen. Blown on the wind, the pollen grains are small enough to slip between the scales and enter each ovule.

Closed Austrian pine cone

Male and female cones

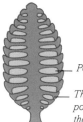

The tough scales enclose ovules, which form on thin scales inside.

Pollen sac

Ovule

These soft scales carry pollen sacs that contain the pollen grains.

Male cone

Female cone

Most conifer trees have separate male and female cones. The long, soft male cones produce pollen, while the woody female cones contain ovules that will become seeds when fertilized. The pollen grains are tiny, like dust, so they are easily blown on the wind.

Other cone-bearing trees

Cycads Sometimes living for 1,000 years, these slow-growing, palmlike plants develop structures called strobili, which are similar to conifer cones.

Welwitschia Found only in the Namib Desert in Africa, these plants are either male or female. Although not true conifers, the females have seed-bearing cones.

Ginkgo These trees are either male or female. The males have pollen-bearing cones, but the females produce seeds that swell up to look like the fruits of flowering trees.

Open cone scales ❯ When the seeds inside a cone are ready, dry weather triggers the cones to open up or even fall off the trees, so the wind can blow the seeds away.

Tough, woody scales grow all around the cone. They open slightly to allow fertilization, and then close again to protect the developing seeds.

Cross-section of a female cone

Seed ❯ Conifer seeds can take up to two years to mature. They are attached to thin scales that act like wings, allowing the seeds to be carried away in the wind when the time is right.

Winged seed

Open Austrian pine cone

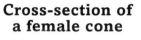

Pines and needles

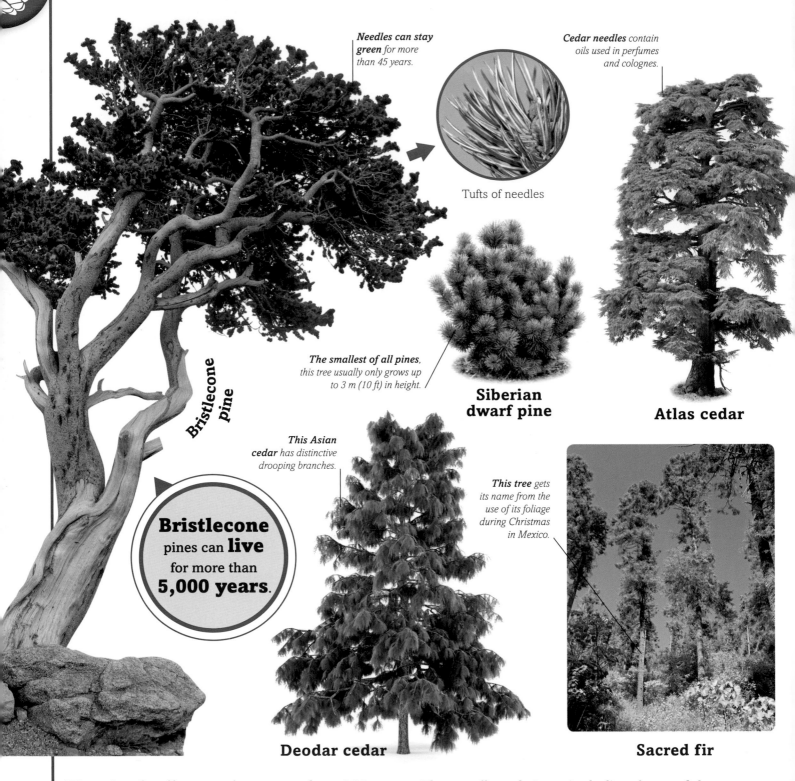

*Needles can stay **green** for more than 45 years.*

Cedar needles contain oils used in perfumes and colognes.

Tufts of needles

Bristlecone pine

The smallest of all pines, this tree usually only grows up to 3 m (10 ft) in height.

Siberian dwarf pine

Atlas cedar

Bristlecone pines can **live** for more than **5,000 years**.

This Asian cedar has distinctive drooping branches.

This tree gets its name from the use of its foliage during Christmas in Mexico.

Deodar cedar

Sacred fir

The pine family contains more than 200 types of conifer trees, including pines, firs, spruces, larches, and cedars. Although they may look similar, these cone-bearing trees have distinct patterns of needlelike leaves that can be used to tell them apart.

The needles of pines, including those of the **bristlecone pine** and **sugar pine**, grow in clusters of two to five – each cluster from a single bud. Cedar needles, such as those of the **Lebanon cedar**, also grow in clusters, but these may contain 15–45 needles and are typically

Young silver fir trees are often used as Christmas trees in Europe.

Sharply pointed needles

This slow-growing but resilient tree has a lifespan of 150–600 years.

Blue spruce

European silver fir

This wide-spreading tree can reach up to 40 m (130 ft) in height. It is the national emblem of Lebanon and appears on its flag.

Whorls of needles

Lebanon cedar

Needles grow in bunches of five, and can be 11 cm (4 in) long.

Short needles turn golden yellow and orange in autumn.

Tamarack larch

This tall tree can grow rapidly, reaching more than 95 m (310 ft) in height.

Sitka spruce

Sugar pine

shorter than pine needles. Firs, such as the **European silver fir**, have flat needles that grow individually from the branch. Spruces, including the **blue spruce** and the **sitka spruce**, have sharp four-sided needles. Larch needles are particularly unusual because,

unlike most conifers, they are not evergreen but deciduous. In autumn, the light blue-green needles of the **tamarack larch** change colour before falling off, turning the wooded mountains glorious golden colours.

Conifer cones

Monkey puzzle tree (male)

Male pollen cones grow up to 15 cm (6 in) in length.

Lodgepole pine

Tightly closed woody cones face down on branches.

These giant cones can weigh up to 5 kg (11 lb).

Female cones produce seeds about 18 months after pollination.

Wollemi pine (female)

Young red cones turn brown before releasing seeds.

European larch

Coulter pine

Red female cones sometimes grow 50 cm (19¾ in) long.

Zululand cycad

Male cones can take up to a year to ripen, turn brown, and release pollen.

Each of these small yellow cones produces a single seed.

Thick, leathery leaves change colour from bronze to green as they mature.

Round, green cones turn purple when ripe.

Outeniqua yellowwood

Kauri (male)

Common juniper

Conifer trees bear cones instead of flowers. All conifers have separate male and female cones, which sometimes grow on different trees. Male cones make pollen while female cones, when pollinated, produce seeds. Cones come in many shapes, sizes, and colours, but all are pollinated by wind.

Conifers have a few tricks for dispersing their seeds. Some, such as the **Outeniqua yellowwood** and **common juniper**, make fleshy, berrylike cones. Birds eat the cones and spread the seeds in their droppings. Other conifers need specific conditions for seed dispersal.

CONE SIZE

The sugar pine grows the world's longest conifer cones – more than four times longer than a human hand.

66 cm (26 in)

Pineapple zamia

Green cones produce bright orange seeds.

The pink female cones of this spruce are 15 cm (6 in) tall and the largest of the spruces.

Sugar pine (wet)

Sugar pine (dry)

Scales open in dry conditions to release winged seeds up to 4 cm (1½ in) long.

Norway spruce (female)

These blue female cones stand upright on top of branches.

Korean fir

Cones may have **"armoured up"** to prevent dinosaurs from eating them.

Colourful pollen cones are only 2 cm (⁴/₅ in) long.

Atlas cedar (male)

Pitch pine (male)

This soft-scaled cone grows up to 8 cm (3 in) long.

The female cones of the **kauri** break apart and release seeds when mature, while **lodgepole pine** cones do not open until they feel the strong heat of a fire. The female cones of the **sugar pine** open only in dry weather, so their light seeds are blown far and wide without moisture in the air weighing them down.

FLOWERING PLANTS

What is a flower?

Many plants rely on animals, such as bees and hummingbirds, to help them reproduce. To attract these animals, many plants have flowers that are brightly coloured, have a sweet scent, and produce a sugary nectar for them to eat. When the animal visits the flower to find the nectar, it becomes covered in pollen. The animal, known as a pollinator, then transports the pollen to another flower.

Stigma ❯ This is the female part of the flower and has either a sticky tip or fine hairs to trap pollen.

Pollen ❯ The fine yellow grains of pollen, found on a tubular structure called an anther, contain the plant's male sex cells.

Stamen ❯ Each stamen has a long filament with an anther on the top where the pollen is produced.

Petals ❯ Colourful, often scented, petals attract pollinating animals to the flower. Petals come in all shapes and sizes, and often look brighter to insect eyes than to human eyes.

Fertilization

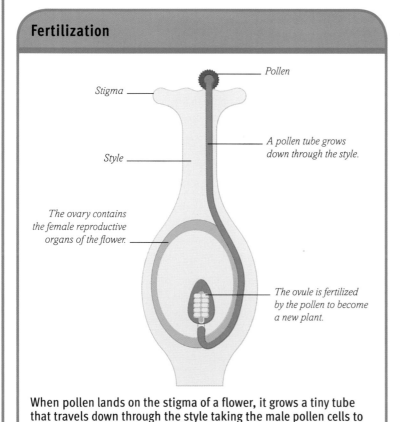

Stigma

Style

The ovary contains the female reproductive organs of the flower.

Pollen

A pollen tube grows down through the style.

The ovule is fertilized by the pollen to become a new plant.

When pollen lands on the stigma of a flower, it grows a tiny tube that travels down through the style taking the male pollen cells to the ovary. Here, the male cells join with female cells in the ovules, which will become the seeds. This process is called fertilization.

Pollination

A tiger lily has colourful petals and sugary nectar for animals such as this bee to eat. As it feeds, the bee brushes against the pollen, which sticks to its body. Pollen contains male cells. When the bee visits another tiger lily, the pollen will brush onto the new flower's stigma, and grow towards the female cells. This is called pollination.

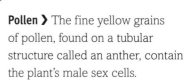

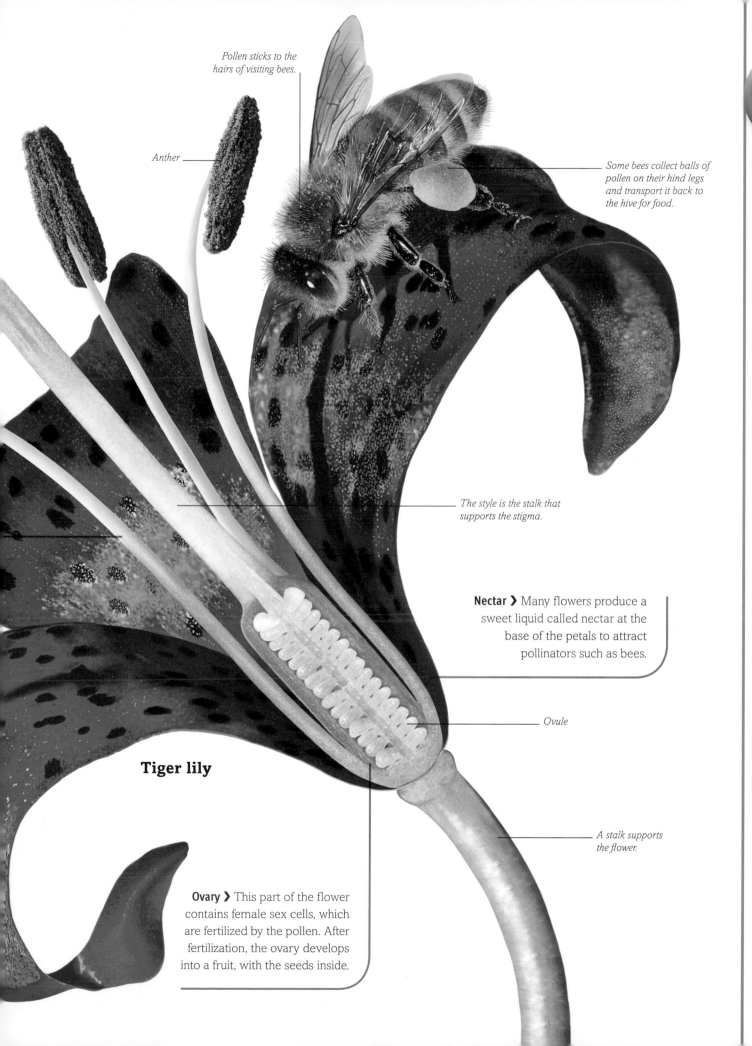

Pollen sticks to the hairs of visiting bees.

Anther

Some bees collect balls of pollen on their hind legs and transport it back to the hive for food.

The style is the stalk that supports the stigma.

Nectar > Many flowers produce a sweet liquid called nectar at the base of the petals to attract pollinators such as bees.

Ovule

Tiger lily

A stalk supports the flower.

Ovary > This part of the flower contains female sex cells, which are fertilized by the pollen. After fertilization, the ovary develops into a fruit, with the seeds inside.

Flower forms

Red powderpuff

Spherical

Red stamens make the flower look like a fluffy pompom.

Frangipani

Rosate

The sweet-smelling frangipani is used to make flower necklaces in Hawaii.

Bird-of-paradise

Orange and purple flowers attract sunbirds, which stand on the thick green perch to access the sweet nectar.

Foxglove

The flower buds at the top open last.

Spots inside the **foxglove flowers** guide bees to the **nectar**.

Irregular

Pale yellow flowers bloom all over Europe during spring.

Primrose

Bell-shaped

Flat-topped tube

A green, beaklike bract protects the flowers.

Wax plant

Thick, waxy petals can withstand tropical storms.

Star-shaped

Plants have flowers that come in a variety of sizes and colours. Botanists (plant scientists) study a flower's shape to better understand how it may be pollinated, by bees, bats, birds, or a breeze!

Some plants, such as **primrose**, **frangipani**, and **poppy,** have simple, open flower shapes that are perfect for a quick visit from an insect. Others make dense clusters of flowers called inflorescences to provide more of a meal for pollinators. For example, the **red powderpuff**

The delicate flower has a lovely, sweet fragrance.

Pea-shaped

Sweet pea

King protea

Small flowers fill the centre of these massive blooms, which can grow up to 30 cm (12 in) across.

Composite

Arum lily

A spike of tiny yellow flowers is surrounded by a white, petal-like bract.

Spadix

Cream-coloured flower spikes are up to 11 cm (4 in) across.

Guelder rose

Pink quill

Red hot poker

Four large petals form a cup shape.

Poppy

Cup-shaped

Purple flowers grow from the edges of the pink bracts.

The stem of the guelder rose is smooth, not thorny like a true rose plant.

Funnel-shaped

A hairy bud protects the growing flower.

Tube-shaped

Saucer-shaped

The petals change colour from orange to yellow as they open.

makes a ball of tiny stamens to attract bees and butterflies, while the **king protea** and **red hot poker** coat the faces of visiting birds with a dusting of pollen when they feed. The **bird-of-paradise** also provides a feast for visiting birds, covering their feet with pollen as they perch on the flower. Other plants make a special, often colourful, petal-like leaf called a bract, to attract many pollinators. Hummingbirds are drawn to the showy bracts of the **pink quill**, while the white bract of the **arum lily** attracts many insects.

Pollinators

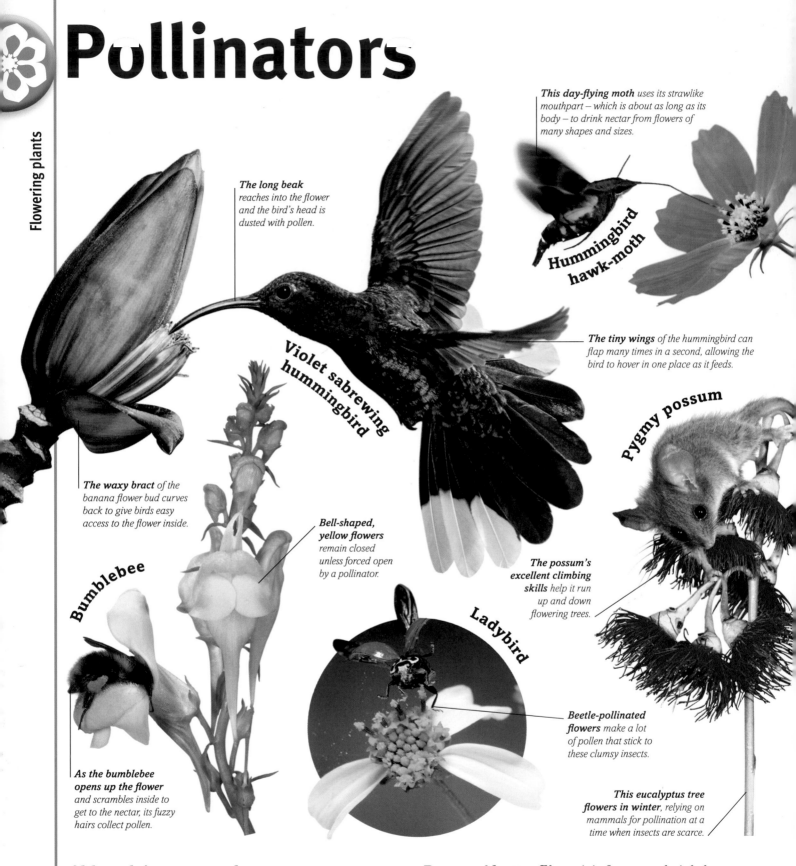

This day-flying moth uses its strawlike mouthpart – which is about as long as its body – to drink nectar from flowers of many shapes and sizes.

Hummingbird hawk-moth

The long beak reaches into the flower and the bird's head is dusted with pollen.

The tiny wings of the hummingbird can flap many times in a second, allowing the bird to hover in one place as it feeds.

Violet sabrewing hummingbird

Pygmy possum

The waxy bract of the banana flower bud curves back to give birds easy access to the flower inside.

Bell-shaped, yellow flowers remain closed unless forced open by a pollinator.

The possum's excellent climbing skills help it run up and down flowering trees.

Bumblebee

Ladybird

As the bumblebee opens up the flower and scrambles inside to get to the nectar, its fuzzy hairs collect pollen.

Beetle-pollinated flowers make a lot of pollen that stick to these clumsy insects.

This eucalyptus tree flowers in winter, relying on mammals for pollination at a time when insects are scarce.

Although insects are the most common pollinators, larger animals such as birds and bats also play a vital role in pollination. In return, plants provide sweet nectar. Different flower shapes, colours, and smells attract specific pollinators.

Bees and butterflies visit fragrant, brightly coloured flowers, which grow in clusters or have large petals for the insects to land on. Many moths prefer white or very pale flowers that open at night, following their sweet floral scents to find them in the dark. Beetles, such

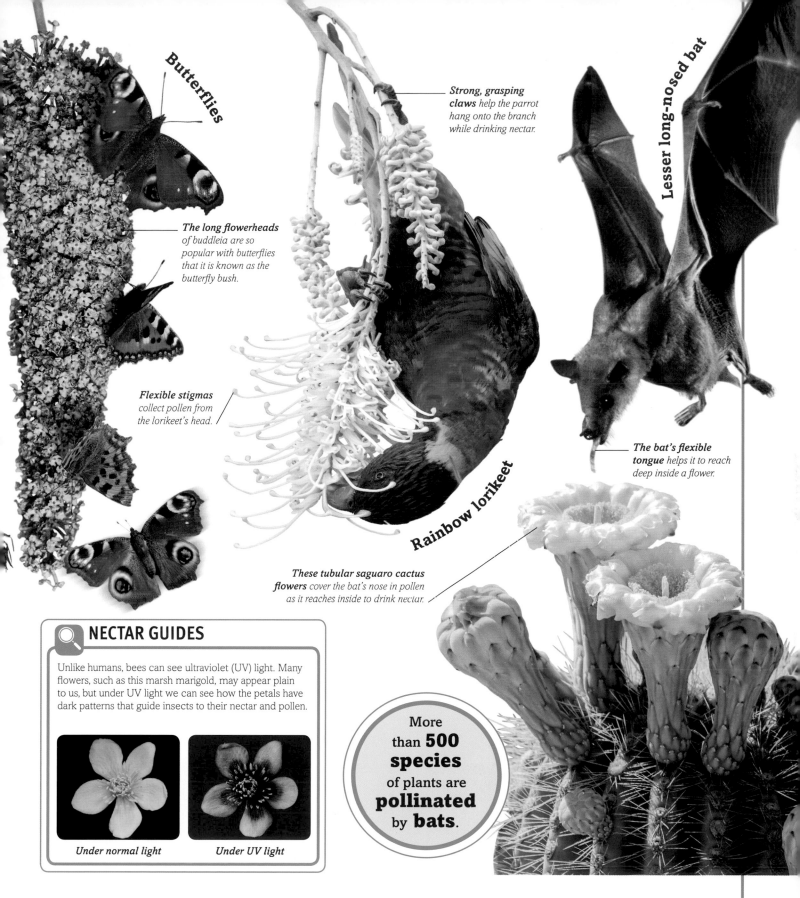

Butterflies

The long flowerheads *of buddleia are so popular with butterflies that it is known as the butterfly bush.*

Flexible stigmas *collect pollen from the lorikeet's head.*

Strong, grasping claws *help the parrot hang onto the branch while drinking nectar.*

Lesser long-nosed bat

The bat's flexible tongue *helps it to reach deep inside a flower.*

Rainbow lorikeet

These tubular saguaro cactus flowers *cover the bat's nose in pollen as it reaches inside to drink nectar.*

🔍 NECTAR GUIDES

Unlike humans, bees can see ultraviolet (UV) light. Many flowers, such as this marsh marigold, may appear plain to us, but under UV light we can see how the petals have dark patterns that guide insects to their nectar and pollen.

Under normal light

Under UV light

More than **500 species** of plants are **pollinated** by **bats**.

as **ladybirds**, also pollinate pale-coloured flowers, but choose fruity-smelling blooms. These flowers mimic the scent of ripe fruit to trick beetles into visiting them for food. Of the larger pollinators, birds are attracted to bright, day-flowering blossoms. **Hummingbirds** favour reddish flowers, but these tend not to be scented, as birds do not have a sense of smell. The petals of bird-pollinated flowers are usually bent back to allow the animals easy access. **Bats** pollinate some night-flowering plants, and are attracted to large, pale flowers with a musty smell.

Looks familiar

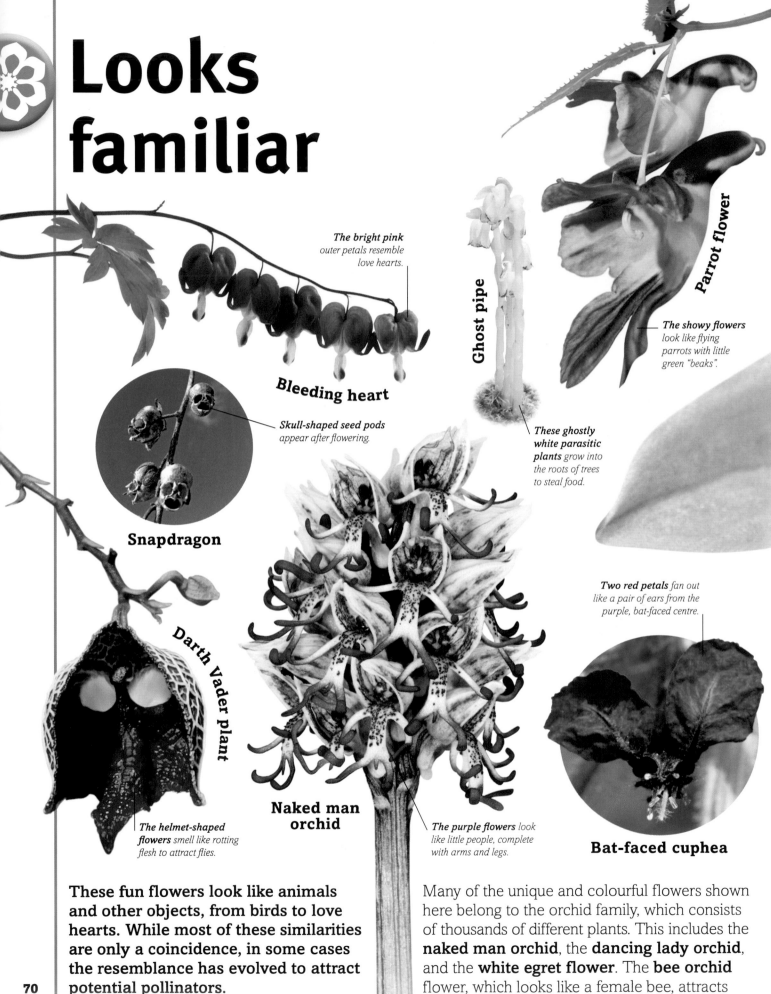

The bright pink outer petals resemble love hearts.

Bleeding heart

Skull-shaped seed pods appear after flowering.

Snapdragon

Ghost pipe

These ghostly white parasitic plants grow into the roots of trees to steal food.

Parrot flower

The showy flowers look like flying parrots with little green "beaks".

Two red petals fan out like a pair of ears from the purple, bat-faced centre.

Darth Vader plant

Naked man orchid

The helmet-shaped flowers smell like rotting flesh to attract flies.

The purple flowers look like little people, complete with arms and legs.

Bat-faced cuphea

These fun flowers look like animals and other objects, from birds to love hearts. While most of these similarities are only a coincidence, in some cases the resemblance has evolved to attract potential pollinators.

Many of the unique and colourful flowers shown here belong to the orchid family, which consists of thousands of different plants. This includes the **naked man orchid**, the **dancing lady orchid**, and the **white egret flower**. The **bee orchid** flower, which looks like a female bee, attracts

A bee orchid's **fragrance** can **trick** a male bee into thinking it is meeting a **female**.

These masses of pollen stick to the bee's head, to be transferred to the next flower.

The delicate white petals resemble the outstretched wings of a heronlike white bird called an egret.

White egret flower

The red leaflike bracts attract hummingbirds to pollinate the flowers inside.

Hot lips

Bee orchid

The pink sepals look like wings and the flower even has a fuzzy, "hairy" body like a bee.

The duck's "head" curls down over visiting insects to deposit pollen on them.

The large, ruffled petal of this chocolate-scented flower looks like a dancer's gown.

The labellum, or lip, traps pollinating insects.

Dancing lady orchid

Large duck orchid

Looks familiar

male bees, attaching packages of pollen to them in the process. The **large duck orchid** looks more like a female sawfly than a duck to male sawflies, luring these pollinators. While many of these eye-catching plants are popular with gardeners, too great a market demand can place a strain on rarer species. For this reason, the government of Thailand has banned the export of the rare **parrot flower** plant and its seeds to protect its dwindling numbers in the wild.

RIVER OF BLOSSOM

A bird's-eye view of Inokashira Park in Tokyo, Japan, reveals the waters of the pond running through it are pink with the petals of the spectacular cherry trees that line its banks. Families and friends take picnics to the park and sit beneath the trees to eat, drink, listen to music, and enjoy the beauty of the blossoms. Later, lanterns hung in the branches are lit, and festivities carry on into the night.

At the start of every year, the Japanese weather office monitors the temperature and conditions to try and predict when the cherry trees, called *sakura*, will bloom. The trees blossom first in the warmer south of Japan, and the "blossom front" spreads up the country, moving north as spring advances. The blossom forecasts are important because thousands of people celebrate flower-viewing parties, a Japanese tradition, known as *hanami*, that dates back to the 8th century. The trees will only carry their blossoms for a week or two and people need to plan their festivities. In Japanese culture, the cherry tree's short-lived bloom is often associated with the fragility of human life.

A garden of roses

Rose-covered arches *bloom in this beautiful garden in Baden-Baden, Germany.*

Rose Garden

Seeds inside the rose hip are eaten by birds attracted by the red fruit, and spread in their droppings.

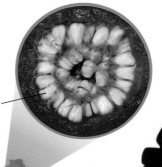

Banks' rose

This climbing rose is native to China.

The crimson rose becomes more fragrant in the warmth of the Sun.

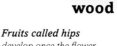

Munstead wood

This full blooming variety was bred from five-petalled wild roses.

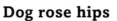

Sunblest rose

Dog rose hips

Fruits called hips develop once the flower has been fertilized and the petals fall off.

Cupped golden yellow petals are mildly scented.

Chinese rose

SPACE ROSE

In 1998, researchers sent the miniature rose they called "Overnight Scentsation" into space, aboard NASA's Space Shuttle *Discovery*. The purpose was to study the effect of low gravity on the oils released from the rose's petals. After 10 days, they discovered that the rose had produced an entirely new scent, unlike any rose scent found on Earth.

Long, straight stems hold these medium- to large-sized roses upright.

Roses were the first plants to be grown simply for their beauty, and have graced gardens for around 5,000 years. The rose flower has been used as a symbol across the world, representing ideas such as love and purity, as well as adopted as the emblem of kings and countries.

Almost all wild roses have five overlapping petals and are known as "single" blooms. Over the centuries, gardeners have taken species of wild roses, particularly the **Chinese rose**, and cultivated them to get flowers with three or more layers of petals, known as "double" blooms, such as the

Making rose oil, Bulgaria

This multi-layered rose variety cost £3 million to develop.

Rose petals must be steamed with water, the same day they are picked, to extract the perfumed oil.

Juliet rose

This pale pink rose is prized for its smell.

Musk rose

This striped pink flower was cultivated more than 400 years ago.

Pale pink flowers bloom from dark pink buds.

Rosa Mundi

Some **rose prickles** can be made into **fishing hooks**.

Leaflike sepals protect the growing bud.

Iceberg was voted the "world's favourite rose" in 1983.

Dog rose

Iceberg rose

Crimson glory

This deep red rose may have as many as 26–40 petals, and is very fragrant.

Banks' rose and **iceberg rose**. Some modern varieties, including the **Juliet rose** and **crimson glory**, have more than 25 petals and are called "full" blooms. Rose breeders have been able to create white, yellow, orange, pink, and red roses, but never a truly blue one. Rose petals contain oils with a wonderful fragrance used in perfumes and many other beauty products, while rose water is used to flavour sweets such as Turkish delight. Some roses, such as the **dog rose**, bear glossy, seed-bearing fruits called rose hips in autumn. Rich in vitamin C, these can be used in teas, preserves, and medicines.

Crazy for daisies

With nearly 25,000 species, daisies make up one of the largest plant families. But their pretty flowerheads are not quite what they seem. What looks like one flower is in fact a cluster of lots – sometimes thousands – of tiny flowers in the centre, with a ring of what looks like petals, but is in fact more flowers around the edge.

Coneflower

Pink petals surround a spiny conelike centre that is full of nectar.

Treasure flower

The striped ray florets surround a centre of tiny disc florets.

Orange pompoms are made of individual flowers and colourful hairs.

Stifftia

Tubular flowers are produced by this critically endangered Hawaiian plant.

Yellow-tipped red florets, which look like flames, give this plant the name "firewheel".

Blanket flower

Maui island-aster

The round flower head is made up of small flowers, ranging from purple to metallic-blue.

The spiky **globe thistle** is also called the **blue hedgehog**.

Three separate florets look like a single flower.

Globe thistle

Whorl flower

76

Daisies such as the **treasure flower**, the **common daisy**, and **chicory** have large outer petal-like ray florets, surrounding the disc florets in the centre. Each disc floret is in fact five petals joined together to form a tubelike flower, seen clearly in the **whorl flower**. The **sunflower** has a large head so you can make out the individual disc florets as they bloom, from the outside in.

Each floret produces one seed. The flower-packed heads of daisies make them much more attractive to insects, and makes pollination easier. Most daisies are brightly coloured to attract insect pollinators, such as bees, but the tropical **Mutisia** flower is pollinated by birds. The other tropical daisies, **stifftia** and the **Maui island-aster**, are unusual because they grow on trees.

The largest sunflower head ever grown was in 1983, at 82 cm (32¼ in) across.

Mutisia

Each petal-like ray floret is a lopsided flower.

The orange ray florets attract bird pollinators.

Sunflower

Yellow disc florets at the centre produce pollen and make seeds.

Edible blue flowers, which are bitter in taste, can be eaten in salads.

Chicory

The purple florets fade to cream towards the centre of the flower head.

Persian cornflower

Common daisy

Ingenious orchids

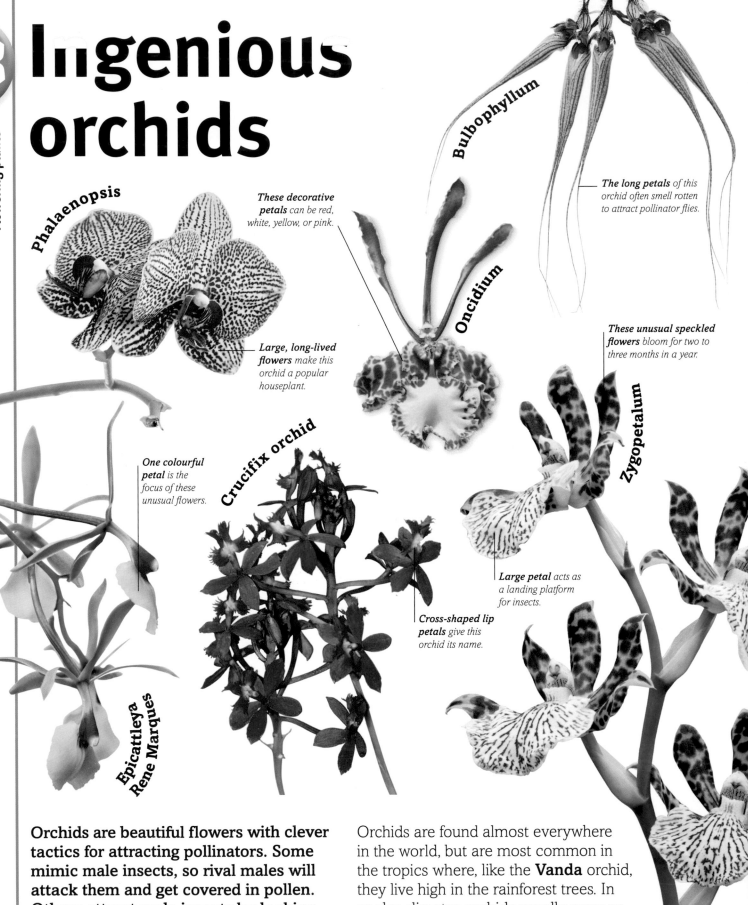

Bulbophyllum

The long petals *of this orchid often smell rotten to attract pollinator flies.*

Phalaenopsis

These decorative **petals** *can be red, white, yellow, or pink.*

Oncidium

Large, long-lived **flowers** *make this orchid a popular houseplant.*

These unusual speckled **flowers** *bloom for two to three months in a year.*

Zygopetalum

One colourful **petal** *is the focus of these unusual flowers.*

Crucifix orchid

Large petal *acts as a landing platform for insects.*

Cross-shaped lip **petals** *give this orchid its name.*

Epicattleya Rene Marques

Orchids are beautiful flowers with clever tactics for attracting pollinators. Some mimic male insects, so rival males will attack them and get covered in pollen. Others attract male insects by looking like females. Some flowers entice bees and butterflies with a sweet smell, while others stink of rotting meat to draw flies.

Orchids are found almost everywhere in the world, but are most common in the tropics where, like the **Vanda** orchid, they live high in the rainforest trees. In cooler climates orchids usually grow on the ground. All orchids have three outer sepals and three inner petals, including a distinctive lip petal which acts as a

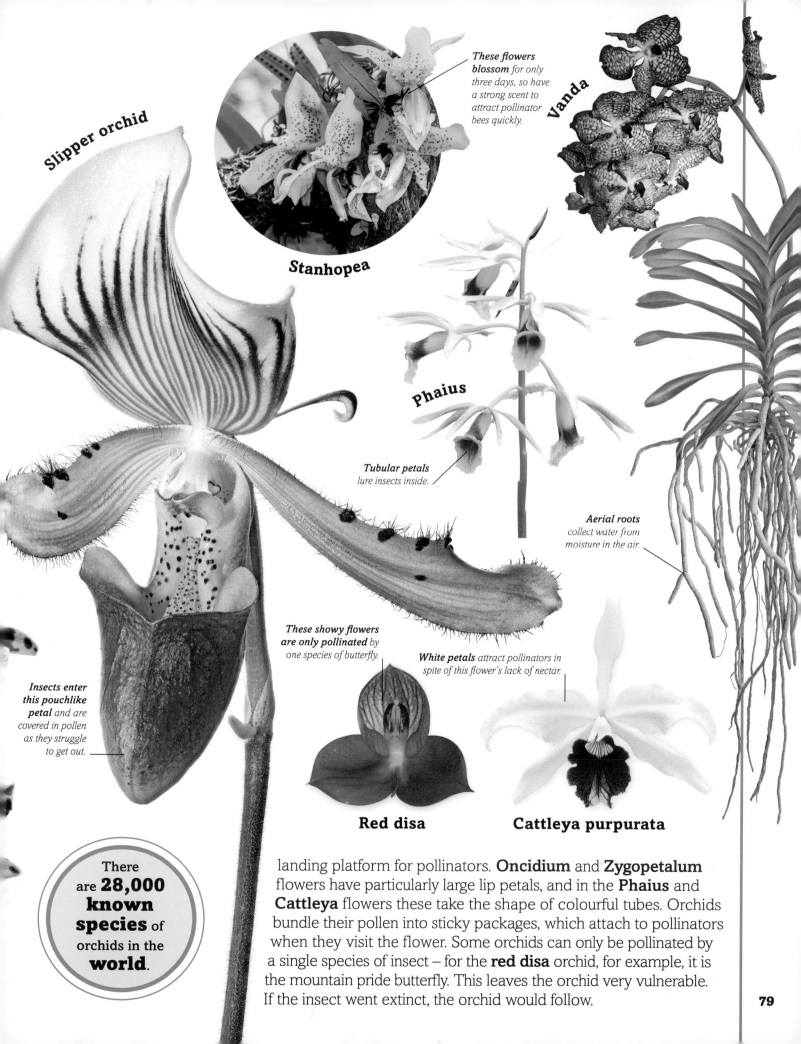

Slipper orchid

Stanhopea

These flowers blossom for only three days, so have a strong scent to attract pollinator bees quickly.

Vanda

Phaius

Tubular petals lure insects inside.

Aerial roots collect water from moisture in the air.

These showy flowers are only pollinated by one species of butterfly.

White petals attract pollinators in spite of this flower's lack of nectar.

Insects enter this pouchlike petal and are covered in pollen as they struggle to get out.

Red disa

Cattleya purpurata

There are **28,000 known species** of orchids in the **world**.

landing platform for pollinators. **Oncidium** and **Zygopetalum** flowers have particularly large lip petals, and in the **Phaius** and **Cattleya** flowers these take the shape of colourful tubes. Orchids bundle their pollen into sticky packages, which attach to pollinators when they visit the flower. Some orchids can only be pollinated by a single species of insect – for the **red disa** orchid, for example, it is the mountain pride butterfly. This leaves the orchid very vulnerable. If the insect went extinct, the orchid would follow.

Blossoms and bulbs

Pink wood sorrel

Daffodil

Tiny bulbs called bulbils, which are 7–11 mm (¹/₄–⁷/₁₆ in) in size, can grow into new plants.

Large bulbs give rise to yellow, trumpet-shaped blooms.

Large flowers bloom before leaves grow from the bulb.

Amaryllis

This bulb starts flowering about 6–8 weeks after planting.

Amaryllis bulb

Delicate, lilylike flowers are produced on leafless stalks.

Nerine

Each **wild leek** stalk can produce **more than 500** flowers.

This bulb only grows in cool weather during the autumn.

Nerine bulb

UNDERGROUND STORE

A bulb is made up of a short stem that produces layers of fleshy leaves known as scales, which store food and water.

Leaves use sunlight to make food.

An outer layer protects the bulb.

Scales are a type of leaf that stores food.

New leaves grow from the stem.

Short stem connects the roots and shoots.

Roots hold the bulb in the ground.

Cross-section of a bulb

Some of our favourite flowers grow from underground food stores, called bulbs. Packed with food and water, bulbs lie dormant beneath the soil when the weather is either too hot or too cold, hidden from hungry animals. But as soon as conditions are right, they quickly sprout new shoots and leaves.

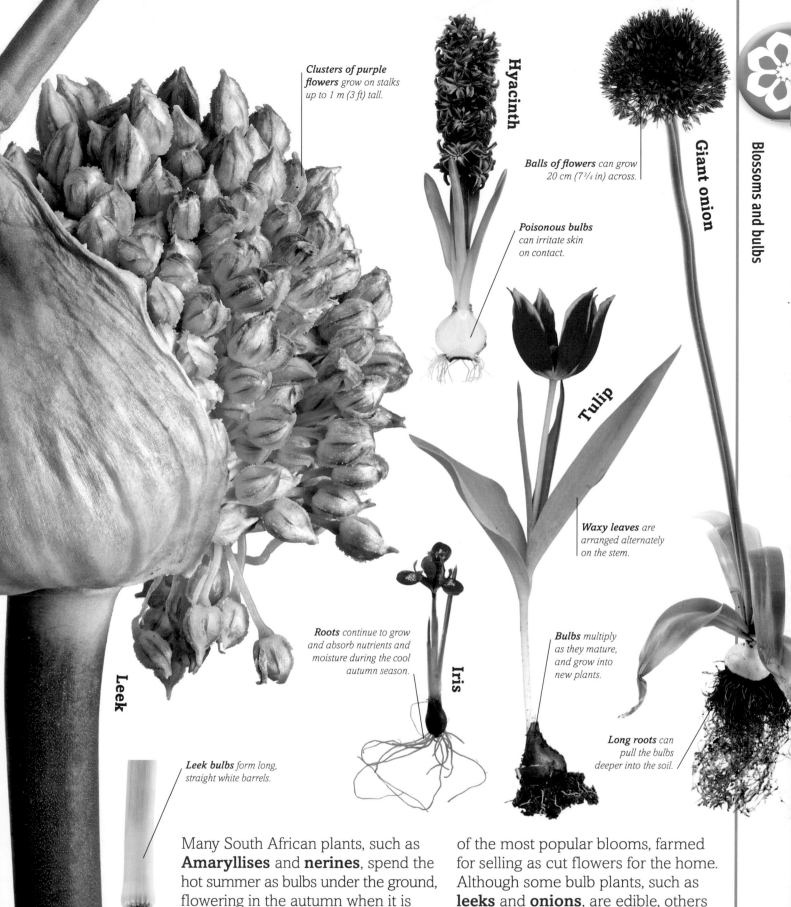

Clusters of purple flowers grow on stalks up to 1 m (3 ft) tall.

Hyacinth

Giant onion

Balls of flowers can grow 20 cm (7 3/4 in) across.

Poisonous bulbs can irritate skin on contact.

Tulip

Waxy leaves are arranged alternately on the stem.

Roots continue to grow and absorb nutrients and moisture during the cool autumn season.

Iris

Bulbs multiply as they mature, and grow into new plants.

Leek

Long roots can pull the bulbs deeper into the soil.

Leek bulbs form long, straight white barrels.

Leek bulb

Many South African plants, such as **Amaryllises** and **nerines**, spend the hot summer as bulbs under the ground, flowering in the autumn when it is cooler. Others, such as **daffodils**, **tulips**, and **hyacinths**, flower in the spring after the cold winter in other countries has ended. These are some of the most popular blooms, farmed for selling as cut flowers for the home. Although some bulb plants, such as **leeks** and **onions**, are edible, others produce toxic chemicals to discourage animals from digging up the bulbs and eating them. Daffodil, hyacinth, and tulip bulbs are poisonous to many animals.

What's that smell?

When we think of flowers, we usually think of the colourful petals and sweet scents that attract pollinators such as bees or butterflies. But some plants smell truly terrible. Their stinking flowers, leaves, and roots attract a different set of pollinators, including flies and beetles.

White blossoms smell like rotting fish to attract flies as pollinators.

Bradford pear

Carrion flowers can grow up to **41 cm** (16 in) across.

The flowers, which bloom in spring and summer, smell like rotting meat to draw in insects.

Pineapple lily

Dragon arum

The star-shaped, hairy flower looks like a dead animal.

Carrion plant

The flower spike may resemble an attractive pineapple, but can smell awful.

Crown imperial

This strange-looking flower traps insects until they are all covered in pollen.

No Durian

Smelly durian fruits are banned on public transport in Singapore.

This plant's brightly coloured blooms, leaves, and stem smell like foxes.

Jackal food

Some flowers, such as those of the **Bradford pear** and **carrion plant**, smell like rotting meat to attract flies. **Jackal food** plants spend most of their lives underground, sending up a poo-scented flower to be pollinated by dung beetles. The **crown imperial** plant, however, uses smell to scare off would-be attackers, such as squirrels and deer, by stinking like a fox or a skunk. Not only do plants such as the **dead horse arum** and **titan arum** smell awful, they also heat up their flowers to help this smell spread farther. The vomitlike smells of the **durian** fruit and female **ginkgo** nut are so strong that both are banned from many public places in some countries.

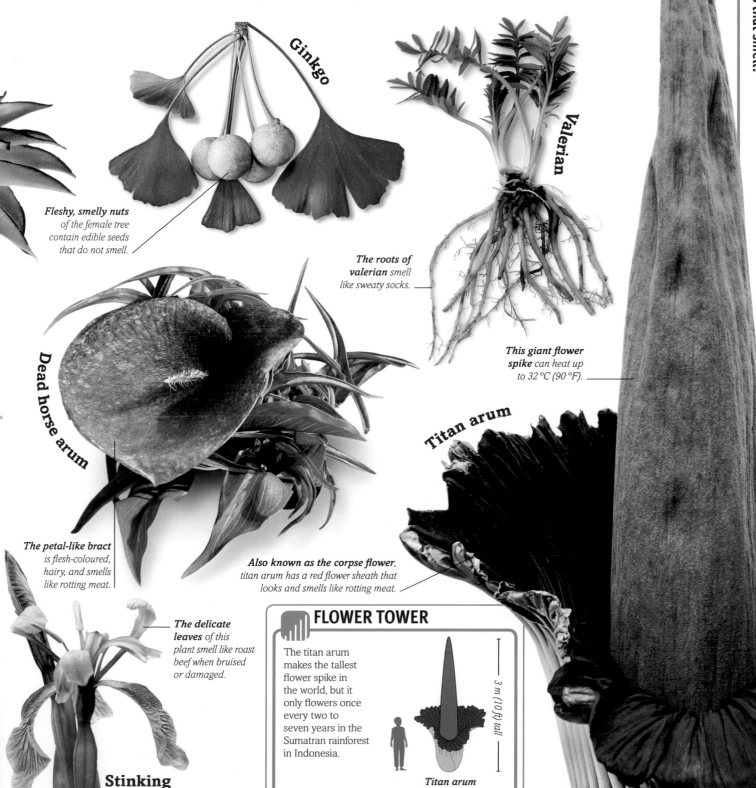

Ginkgo

Fleshy, smelly nuts *of the female tree contain edible seeds that do not smell.*

Valerian

The roots of valerian *smell like sweaty socks.*

Dead horse arum

This giant flower spike *can heat up to 32 °C (90 °F).*

Titan arum

The petal-like bract *is flesh-coloured, hairy, and smells like rotting meat.*

Also known as the corpse flower, *titan arum has a red flower sheath that looks and smells like rotting meat.*

The delicate leaves *of this plant smell like roast beef when bruised or damaged.*

Stinking iris

FLOWER TOWER

The titan arum makes the tallest flower spike in the world, but it only flowers once every two to seven years in the Sumatran rainforest in Indonesia.

3 m (10 ft) tall

Titan arum

Living in water

Ponds, rivers, and oceans are full of plants. These often grow quickly because they have access to a lot of water and sunlight. Some aquatic plants float on the surface, their flat leaves soaking up the Sun's rays, while others are fully submerged. Many send up leaves and flowers from an anchored underwater root.

Water hyacinth

Flower spike and leaves reach up to 1.5 m (5 ft) tall.

Waxy lily pads rest on the water's surface.

Flowering rush

Water lily

Air-filled leaf stalks help the plant float.

Fanwort

Fan-shaped leaves give this plant its name.

Stems, not roots, anchor this plant under water.

Hornwort

🔍 LIVING UNDER WATER

All plants need oxygen to survive. Some aquatic plants take in oxygen from the water, while others, such as the water lily, have tiny tubes in their stalks to carry air from above the water's surface to their roots.

Air spaces allow oxygen to pass from the leaves down to the roots.

Water lily

Cross-section of leaf stalk

Just like plants on land, water-based plants need sunlight to make food and have found their own unique ways to survive. Plants such as the **flowering rush** and **water lily** are rooted at the bottom of ponds and rivers, but push out long leaves to capture sunlight, and tall flower stalks to be pollinated by insects. The feathery leaves of the **fanwort** and **hornwort** spread out to let the water drift freely through without tearing them. **Water hyacinths** and **water lettuces** trap air in their leaves to help them float. While some water plants provide a habitat and food for fish and other aquatic animals, others such as **waterweed** and **parrot's feather** grow so quickly that they often take over lakes and streams, harming other plants and the animals that live there.

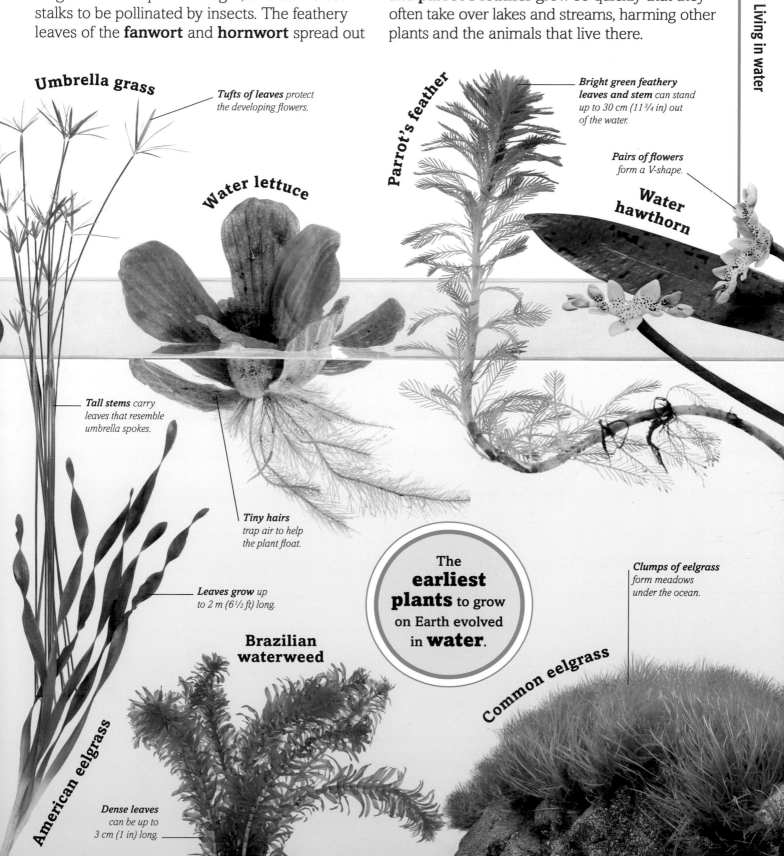

Umbrella grass

Tufts of leaves protect the developing flowers.

Water lettuce

Tall stems carry leaves that resemble umbrella spokes.

Tiny hairs trap air to help the plant float.

Leaves grow up to 2 m (6½ ft) long.

Parrot's feather

Bright green feathery leaves and stem can stand up to 30 cm (11¾ in) out of the water.

Pairs of flowers form a V-shape.

Water hawthorn

The **earliest plants** to grow on Earth evolved in **water**.

American eelgrass

Brazilian waterweed

Dense leaves can be up to 3 cm (1 in) long.

Clumps of eelgrass form meadows under the ocean.

Common eelgrass

Along the river

The soil along a riverbank is rich in nutrients deposited by flooding, so plants here can grow large and often very fast. They thrive all summer long, as they rarely suffer drought. However, when a river floods, the fast-flowing water may carry away any plants not firmly rooted in the soil.

Swamp rose mallow

Each large flower grows to about 15 cm (6 in) across.

Brilliant yellow flowers attract bees in early spring.

Marsh marigold

Giant rhubarb

Tiny, brown female flowers grow in the form of a dense spike.

These huge leaves have a spiny underside that stops animals from eating them.

Bulrush

GIANT LEAVES

Native to riverbanks in Brazil, the giant rhubarb has massive leaves – the largest undivided leaves of any flowering plant. Its flowers, however, are tiny, and grow on spiky heads near the ground.

3.3 m (10⅞ ft)

One of the biggest riverside plants, the **giant rhubarb**, grows 2.5 m (8 ft) tall and 4 m (13 ft) wide. Not much smaller, the **white skunk cabbage** grows huge cabbagelike leaves. Both plants die away in winter, shedding leaves that might otherwise become caught up in floodwater and uproot them. Plants such as the **marsh marigold**, **purple** **loosestrife**, **water spearmint**, and **candelabra primrose** lie dormant in winter, but grow fast in spring or summer. **Bulrush**, **soft rush**, and **snowberry** have a different method of survival. Their tough leaves or stems can withstand swift floodwaters, so each year they grow bigger and stronger.

The brown, conelike structures at the end of this non-flowering plant's stems contain spores.

Stalks of horsetail were used by early American pioneers to scour **pots** and **pans**.

In North America, these white berries are food for bighorn sheep and grizzly bears.

Common snowberry

Clusters of up to six flowers are borne on tall, sturdy stems.

Soft rush

Rough horsetail

Tall spikes of delicate mauve flowers blossom in late summer.

A cluster of bright red flowers grows on the side of the stem.

Purple loosestrife

Candelabra primrose

These leaves have a minty smell.

Large, white leaflike bracts attract flies to the smelly flower heads.

Water spearmint

White skunk cabbage

FLOODED FOREST
A shoal of fish swirl past the tangled roots of a mangrove tree that stands partially submerged in the warm Caribbean Sea off the Central American country of Belize. Most mangroves grow along tropical and subtropical coastlines, where their roots are flooded with seawater twice a day. Such a wet, salty environment would be fatal to most plants, but mangrove forests thrive in it.

Mangroves include everything from small shrubs to huge trees, all adapted for living in salt water. The plants use a range of survival tactics, from filtering out salt in seawater as they drink it in through their roots, to releasing salt through leaf pores. Many mangrove trees stop their roots from rotting by absorbing oxygen through spongy, upright roots at low tide.

Then, at high tide, the pores in their roots close, preventing the trees from getting waterlogged. Mangroves are an important tropical and subtropical habitat, acting as natural storm barriers and preventing coastal erosion. The network of roots is also a source of food for fish and other small ocean creatures, and helps shelter them from larger predators.

What is a cactus?

Cacti come in all shapes and sizes, but nearly all of them have large swollen stems that allow them to store water. This is because many cacti grow in areas with little or no rainfall for long periods of time. Desert cacti have clever adaptations to help them survive extreme heat and drought, however a few very different cacti live in rainforests.

Summer flower ❯ The monk's hood cactus produces pale yellow flowers throughout the summer. They are pollinated by insects and produce spiky fruits.

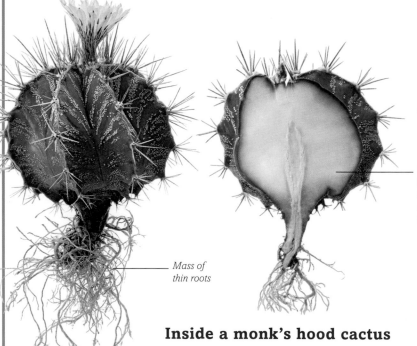

Water is stored in the barrel-shaped stem. Some cacti, such as this one, expand when filled with water and contract when dry.

Mass of thin roots

Inside a monk's hood cactus

Roots ❯ The roots of this cactus spread across a large area and grow close to the surface. They quickly draw in as much water as possible from rain or dew.

Spine > These help to shade the stem and stop animals eating the cactus. A spine is, in fact, a type of modified leaf with a small surface area to prevent water from evaporating.

The ribs channel dew to the roots.

Monk's hood cactus

Flakes > In a desert, the Sun is very bright. White flakes grow on the stem of the cactus, helping to reflect light.

Cacti shapes

Columnar
Cacti, such as the saguaro, can grow 12 m (40 ft) tall, and have distinctive armlike side branches. Bats pollinate their flowers, which grow at the top of the plant.

Clustering
The prickly pear cactus has flattened stems that grow in clusters. The red, prickly fruit must be peeled to remove the small spines.

Globular
Many cacti, like the golden barrel cactus, have rounded stems. This maximizes water storage, while its vertical ridges direct every drop of water to the roots.

Climbing
Some cacti live in forests, where they clamber up other plants for sunlight. The queen of the night cactus has huge flowers that bloom for just one night.

Where do they grow?

Deserts
Desert cacti have to survive extreme heat and light. Often large and spiny, they grow all over North and South America.

Forests
Some cacti grow in shaded forests. Their stems do not need to store water, as the roots draw moisture from the air.

Grasslands
Smaller cacti often grow in grasslands, where the grasses shade them in summer. Most are found in South America.

Cool cacti

Long, yellow spines erupt in starry clusters from ridges on the body.

Vertical stems can grow up to 8 m (26 ft) tall.

Organ pipe cactus

Barrel cactus

Branches can take up to 40 years to form, growing at less than 2.5 cm (1 in) a year.

Overlapping stems create a fan shape.

Saguaro

Bilberry cactus

Paddle-shaped stems are flat, unlike stems in most cacti.

TALLEST CACTUS

With a recorded height of 19.2 m (63 ft) and a trunk about 1 m (3 ft) thick, the Mexican elephant cactus is the tallest-known living cactus in the world.

19.2 m (63 ft)

Birds such as this owl use the saguaro cactus for nesting.

Prickly pear

Many cacti live in the desert, where their water-filled stems help them survive long periods of drought. Most plants use their leaves to make food from sunlight, but cacti do this using their green, fleshy stems. To protect themselves from hungry animals, cacti have specially adapted leaves called spines.

Living in hot and dry environments means that cacti have to make the most of the rare, but often heavy, rainfall. Ribs on the **barrel cactus** allow it to stretch its stem to quickly take in as much water as possible. In harsh desert conditions, plants grow very slowly and live a long time. Some, such as the **saguaro** and **elephant cacti**, can live for up to 300 years. These tall cacti,

Christmas cactus

Flowers bloom around Christmas time in the Northern Hemisphere.

Fragrant flowers grow on top of this rounded cactus.

Fiercely sharp, long spines protect this cactus.

Tephrocactus

White, hairlike spines reduce evaporation.

Old man cactus

Bishop's cap cactus

Red spines give this plant its name.

Mexican fire barrel

Flowers open at night for moth and beetle pollinators.

Neon broom cactus

Elephant cactus

Stout stems can be up to 1 m (3.3 ft) thick.

along with the **organ pipe cactus**, are pollinated by lesser long-nosed bats at night, while most other species are visited by insects or birds during the day. **Prickly pears** curl their anthers around visiting bees to coat them in pollen. Not all cacti live in the desert – the **Christmas cactus**, for example, grows on trees in the tropical rainforests of Brazil.

Desert survivors

Moulded wax

When dry, resurrection plants close down and curl up to preserve moisture.

Dried plant

After rain, the leaves unfurl in a matter of hours.

Resurrection plant

Spiny leaves with sharp tips can grow up to 1.5 m (5 ft) in length.

Shiny, triangular leaves are arranged in a rosette.

Century plant

The high, thorny branches can only be eaten by giraffes, with their muscular tongues.

The dense cushions of leaves of this poisonous plant trap water inside.

Camel thorn

Llareta

A desert is a very dry area, with less than 25 cm (10 in) of rainfall a year. All plants need water to survive, but desert plants have adapted to their habitat by using ingenious methods of storing water, reducing the amount they lose, or just by being able to survive drying out.

The **moulded wax** plant and the **Queen Victoria agave** retain water by trapping it inside their fleshy leaves. Their leaves also have a waxy surface that reflects the Sun's rays and keeps the plant cool. The **resurrection plant** can lose more than 95 per cent of its weight during dry periods, shrivelling into a dry ball. It can survive

Bitter fruits contain fatty seeds used to make oils and biofuels.

Wild desert gourd

The fleshy stem makes food for the plant by photosynthesis.

Now **protected** by law, baseball plants nearly went **extinct** due to over-collecting.

Baseball plant

These white **patterns** mark where growing leaves pushed against each other.

The young leaves of this tree are eaten and sometimes used as medicine in Ethiopia.

Pebblelike leaves camouflage this plant in rocky deserts.

African moringa

Queen Victoria agave

Living stone

like this for several years, but quickly comes back to life when rain soaks its leaves. Like cacti, the **baseball plant**, **living stone**, and **African moringa** store water in their stems. Plants are fairly uncommon in deserts and semi-deserts, so many predators eye them hungrily. The **camel thorn** and **century plant** defend themselves using sharp thorns or spines, while others, including the **llareta**, protect themselves with poison.

DESERT BLOOM
The vast Atacama Desert in Chile is one of the driest places in the world, receiving just a few millimetres of rainfall a year. The bare, baked ground appears bleak and lifeless. When it rains, however, millions of flowering plants, such as these purple pussypaws, spring up and transform the land into a carpet of colour. These short-lived plants, or "ephemerals", grow from seeds that have long lain dormant in the earth.

Desert ephemerals are plants that live fast and die young. Once the right conditions have triggered their explosion of growth, they have a few weeks, or often just days, to complete their life cycle. Ephemerals are usually small and short. Growing tall takes time and energy, and desert plants have none to spare. They must make the most of their short season by producing flowers and setting seed very quickly. With the return of drought, the ephemerals disappear as fast as they came. They leave behind their scattered seeds, safely hidden in cracks in the parched ground, where they sit out the tough times until the next rains. It may be a very long wait.

Meat-eating plants

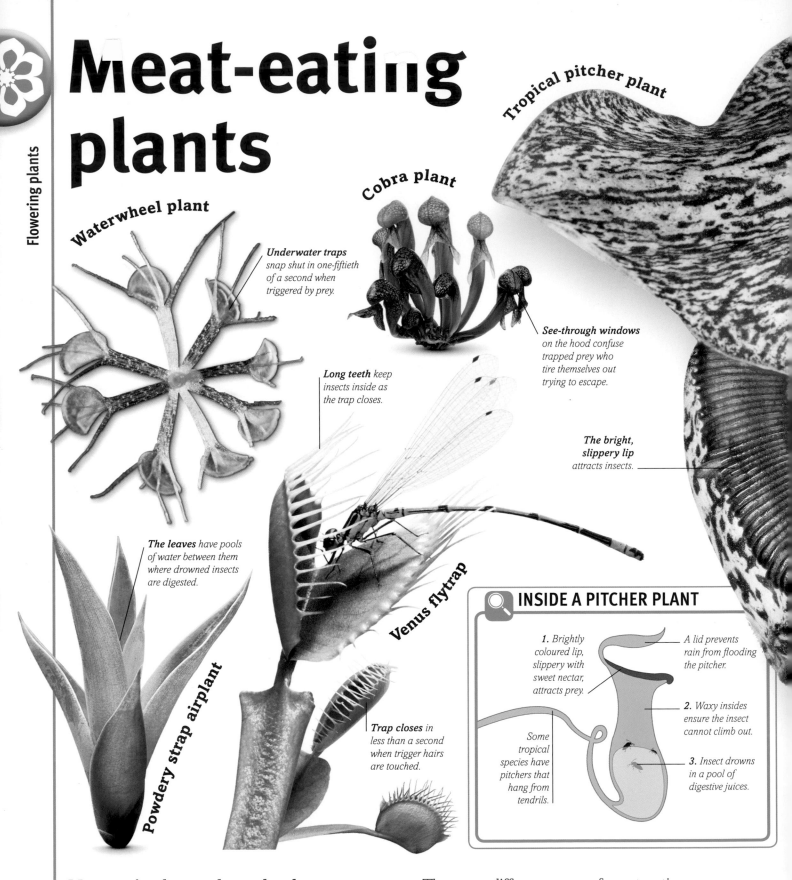

Tropical pitcher plant

Waterwheel plant

Cobra plant

Underwater traps snap shut in one-fiftieth of a second when triggered by prey.

Long teeth keep insects inside as the trap closes.

See-through windows on the hood confuse trapped prey who tire themselves out trying to escape.

The bright, slippery lip attracts insects.

The leaves have pools of water between them where drowned insects are digested.

Venus flytrap

Powdery strap airplant

Trap closes in less than a second when trigger hairs are touched.

INSIDE A PITCHER PLANT

1. Brightly coloured lip, slippery with sweet nectar, attracts prey.

A lid prevents rain from flooding the pitcher.

Some tropical species have pitchers that hang from tendrils.

2. Waxy insides ensure the insect cannot climb out.

3. Insect drowns in a pool of digestive juices.

Many animals eat plants, but have you ever heard of a plant eating an animal? Meat-eating plants often grow in bogs, trapping insects and other small animals to get the nitrogen and minerals they need that are missing from the wet soil.

There are different types of meat-eating, or carnivorous, plants. **Waterwheel plants** and **venus flytraps** have snap traps, which quickly close shut around their victims. **Pitcher plants** have a lip of nectar to attract their prey. The insects then fall into the pitcher (jug) of digestive

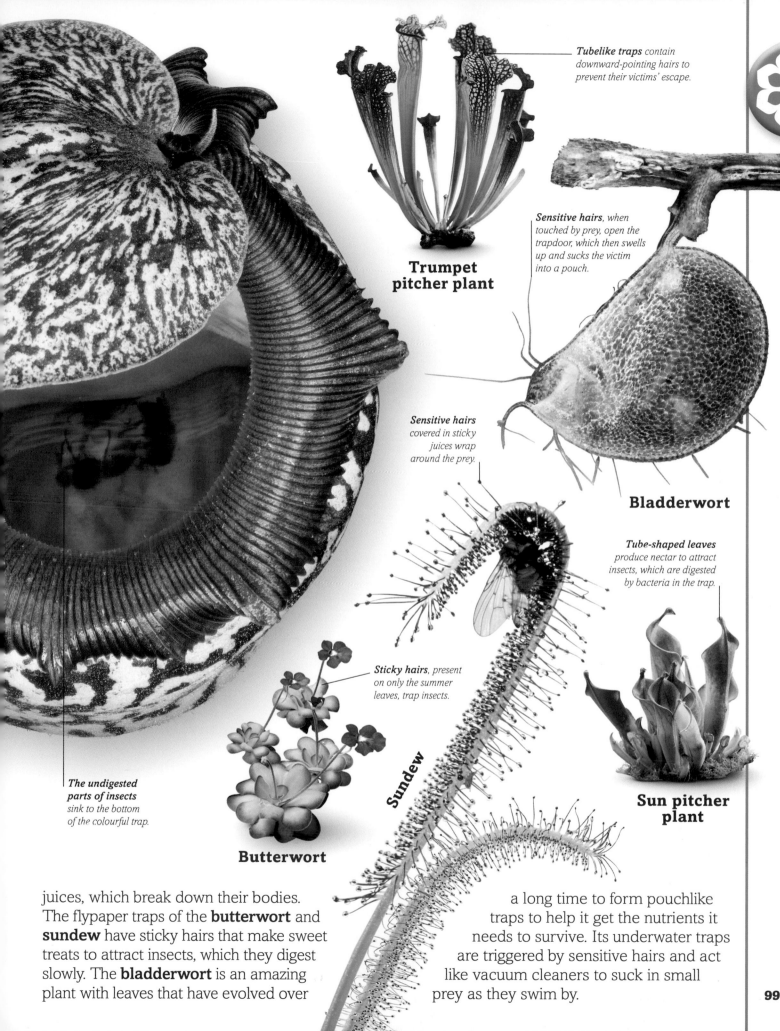

Tubelike traps contain downward-pointing hairs to prevent their victims' escape.

Trumpet pitcher plant

Sensitive hairs, when touched by prey, open the trapdoor, which then swells up and sucks the victim into a pouch.

Bladderwort

Sensitive hairs covered in sticky juices wrap around the prey.

Tube-shaped leaves produce nectar to attract insects, which are digested by bacteria in the trap.

Sticky hairs, present on only the summer leaves, trap insects.

Sundew

Sun pitcher plant

The undigested parts of insects sink to the bottom of the colourful trap.

Butterwort

juices, which break down their bodies. The flypaper traps of the **butterwort** and **sundew** have sticky hairs that make sweet treats to attract insects, which they digest slowly. The **bladderwort** is an amazing plant with leaves that have evolved over a long time to form pouchlike traps to help it get the nutrients it needs to survive. Its underwater traps are triggered by sensitive hairs and act like vacuum cleaners to suck in small prey as they swim by.

Poisonous plants

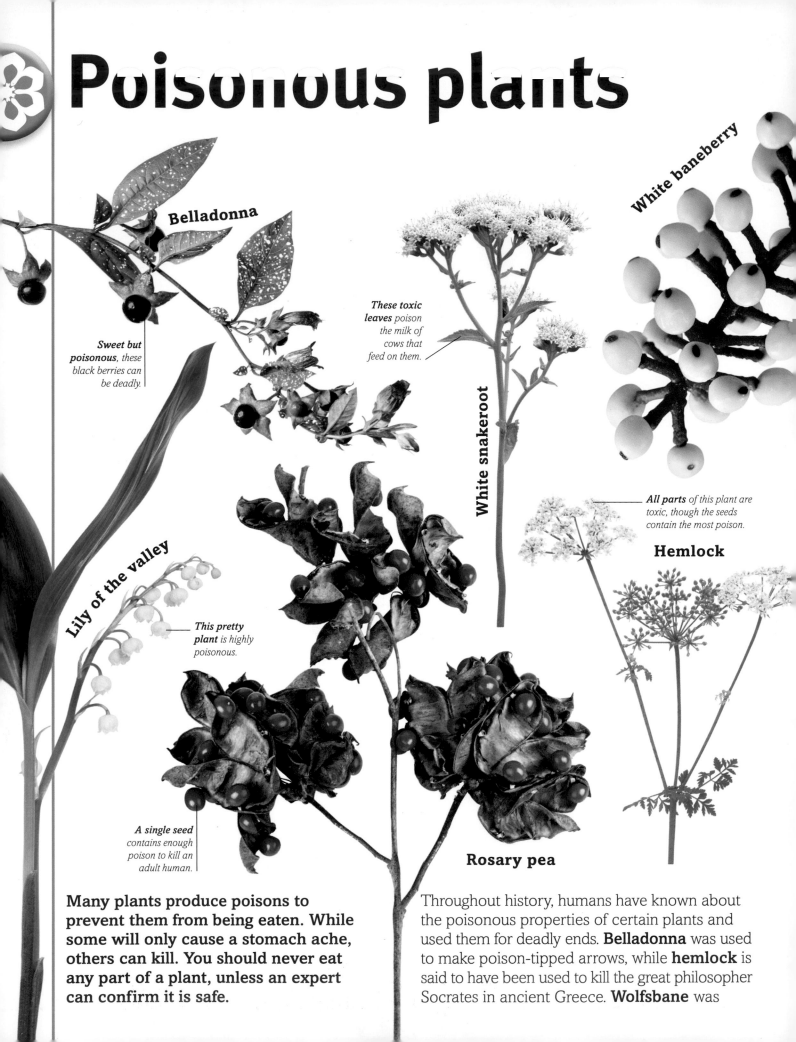

Belladonna

Sweet but poisonous, these black berries can be deadly.

These toxic leaves poison the milk of cows that feed on them.

White snakeroot

White baneberry

All parts of this plant are toxic, though the seeds contain the most poison.

Hemlock

Lily of the valley

This pretty plant is highly poisonous.

A single seed contains enough poison to kill an adult human.

Rosary pea

Many plants produce poisons to prevent them from being eaten. While some will only cause a stomach ache, others can kill. You should never eat any part of a plant, unless an expert can confirm it is safe.

Throughout history, humans have known about the poisonous properties of certain plants and used them for deadly ends. **Belladonna** was used to make poison-tipped arrows, while **hemlock** is said to have been used to kill the great philosopher Socrates in ancient Greece. **Wolfsbane** was

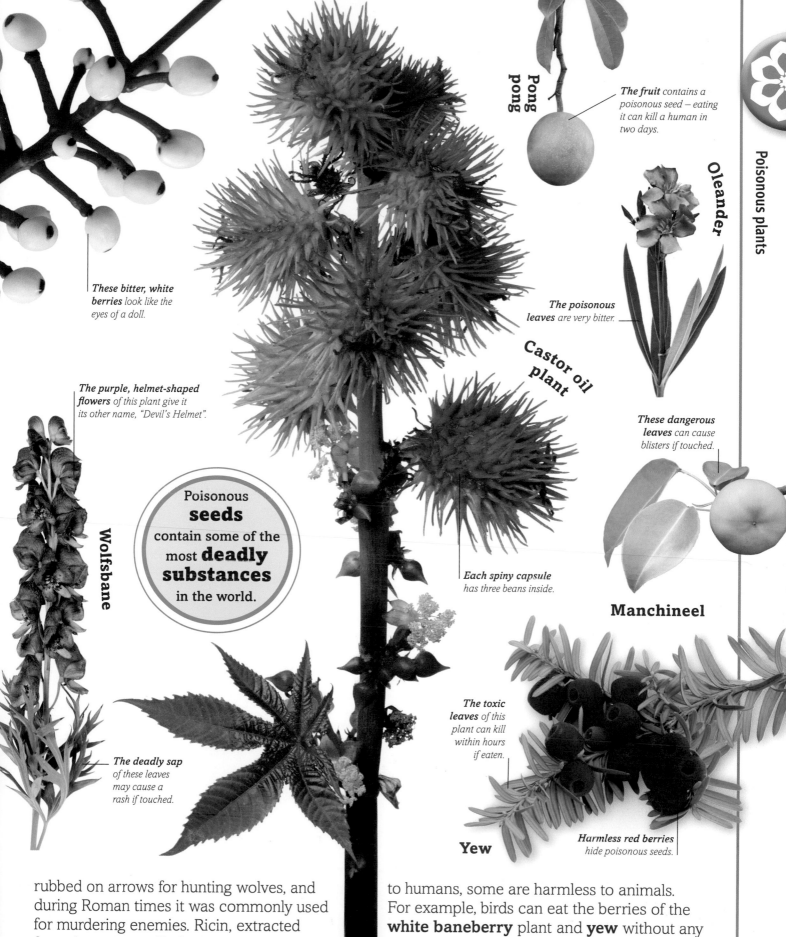

These bitter, white berries look like the eyes of a doll.

Pong pong

The fruit contains a poisonous seed – eating it can kill a human in two days.

Oleander

The poisonous leaves are very bitter.

Castor oil plant

The purple, helmet-shaped flowers of this plant give it its other name, "Devil's Helmet".

These dangerous leaves can cause blisters if touched.

Poisonous **seeds** contain some of the most **deadly substances** in the world.

Wolfsbane

Each spiny capsule has three beans inside.

Manchineel

The deadly sap of these leaves may cause a rash if touched.

The toxic leaves of this plant can kill within hours if eaten.

Yew

Harmless red berries hide poisonous seeds.

rubbed on arrows for hunting wolves, and during Roman times it was commonly used for murdering enemies. Ricin, extracted from the **castor oil plant**, remains one of the most deadly poisons known today. Although all the plants shown here are toxic to humans, some are harmless to animals. For example, birds can eat the berries of the **white baneberry** plant and **yew** without any ill-effects. The birds then spread the seeds in their poo. Iguanas are known to feast on the fruit and leaves of the toxic **manchineel**.

Parasitic plants

Mistletoe

The plants take root on branches, from seeds dropped by birds that eat mistletoe berries.

Dodder

Thin stems wrap around a host plant and weaken its immune system.

Cactus mistletoe

Red flowers are the only part of this leafless parasite that is visible outside the cactus.

The pale stems of this plant are parasites of ivy plants.

Thurber's stemsucker

Mushroom-shaped flower stalks emerge from underground stems, which feed on the roots of host plants.

Helosis

Ivy broomrape

Tiny flowers, 2 mm across, bloom along the host stem.

Most plants absorb water and nutrients from the soil to make their own food using energy from sunlight, but others have developed sneakier ways to survive. Parasitic plants pierce the stems or roots of other plants to steal their hard-earned supplies.

There are two main types of parasitic plant. Hemiparasites (half parasites) can use sunlight to make some of their own food, but absorb water, nutrients, and sometimes sugars from the host plants they live on. Some hemiparasites, such as **mistletoe** and the **Australian Christmas tree**, will

Eyebright

This tiny wildflower relies on nutrients stolen from the roots of nearby grasses.

Butter and eggs

The parasite steals nutrients from the roots of other plants to grow as tall as 35 cm (13⁴/₅ in).

The corpse lily has the world's **largest flower**, more than 1 m (3 ¼ ft) across.

INVADING A HOST

All parasitic plants have modified roots called haustoria, which enter the roots or stems of host plants to steal food, water, and nutrients.

Host plant

Parasite

The haustoria grow towards the chemical signals given off by the host's roots.

Corpse lily

The flowers of this plant look and smell like rotting meat.

Australian Christmas tree

This tree's greedy roots can steal nutrients from plants 110 m (360 ft) away.

die if they cannot find a host to steal from. Others, including **eyebright** and **butter and eggs**, can survive without a host, although they tend to not grow as well. On the other hand, the second type, holoparasites (whole parasites), cannot make any food of their own, and must find a host plant to survive.

Some holoparasites, such as **dodder**, grow above ground. Most, such as the **cactus mistletoe**, **Helosis**, **Thurber's stemsucker**, and the impressive **corpse lily**, live within their host plant, emerging only to flower. Parasitic plants do not generally kill their hosts but can weaken them.

Mountain life

This sugarbush is an endangered plant in its native South Africa.

Serpentine sugarbush

Forget-me-not

The alpine pink's tiny leaves are almost hidden by large flowers in spring.

Many heads of bright yellow flowers burst out of each rosette.

These tightly curled heads of pink buds open into blue flowers.

Alpine pink

The tall flower spikes develop quickly in spring.

Broadleaf stonecrop

Star-shaped flowers attract pollinating bees.

Alpine spotted orchid

Fleshy blue-green leaves are spade-shaped.

Cobweb house-leek

Life up a mountain is harsh. At high altitude, plants are exposed to extreme temperatures, freezing weather in winter, and intense sunlight in summer. The thin soil is dry. Yet some hardy plants manage to survive here. Many have short stems to keep out of the wind, and small leaves to reduce heat and water loss. They usually hug the ground in clumps. Some plants even have silver or white leaves to reflect sunlight.

The spikes of nodding flowers may reach 60 cm (24 in) in height.

Mountain buttercup

This endangered Hawaiian plant grows on the edge of a volcano at more than 2,100 m (6,900 ft). Its swordlike leaves are covered in silver hair.

Haleakala silversword

Spotted fritillary

Some plants can grow **up to 6,150 m** (20,177 ft) above sea level.

This wild plant stays very short to avoid strong winds.

Even the flower heads of the prostrate speedwell grow close to the ground.

Prostrate speedwell

This beautiful plant survives extreme cold, but not drought.

Himalayan may apple

Long-petalled lewisia

Fine white hairs that look like cobwebs reduce heat and water loss.

This rare plant is only found near Lake Tahoe in California, USA.

Mountain plants have adapted to the dry climate of their habitat in different ways. The **alpine spotted orchid** and **spotted fritillary** survive the cold winter as bulbs, flowering in spring. The **Himalayan may apple** cannot tolerate bright, dry conditions, so it grows quickly in spring and then dies back underground for the rest of the year. Others, such as the **broadleaf stonecrop**, **alpine pink**, **cobweb house-leek**, and **long-petalled lewisia** produce short, sturdy leaves, and survive all year by staying close to the ground for protection from the wind.

Creepers and climbers

Star jasmine

Gardeners often grow these fragrant flowers *up a teepee of poles.*

This sweetly scented **climber** *is covered in white flowers.*

Fine tendrils twirl slowly round until they find something to grab onto.

Vines **recognize** their own chemical **signal**, so avoid strangling themselves.

The plant's thorny **stems** *can grow up to 12 m (39 ft) tall.*

Perennial sweet pea

Showers of flowers hang from twining stems.

Bougainvillea

Wisteria

Thorny hooks

Vines can be creepers or climbers. Creepers grow and spread along the ground, while climbers clamber up towards the sunlight. As these vines grow, they may curl around a tree, or up a wall or fence, adding colour to the garden.

Some creepers, such as **jasmine**, twirl their flexible stems around other plants to reach for the sky. **Clematis** plants do the same but use long leaf stalks to wrap around their neighbours in order to climb upwards. **Bougainvillea** hooks its thorns into surfaces to drag itself higher, while **sweet pea**, Virginia creeper,

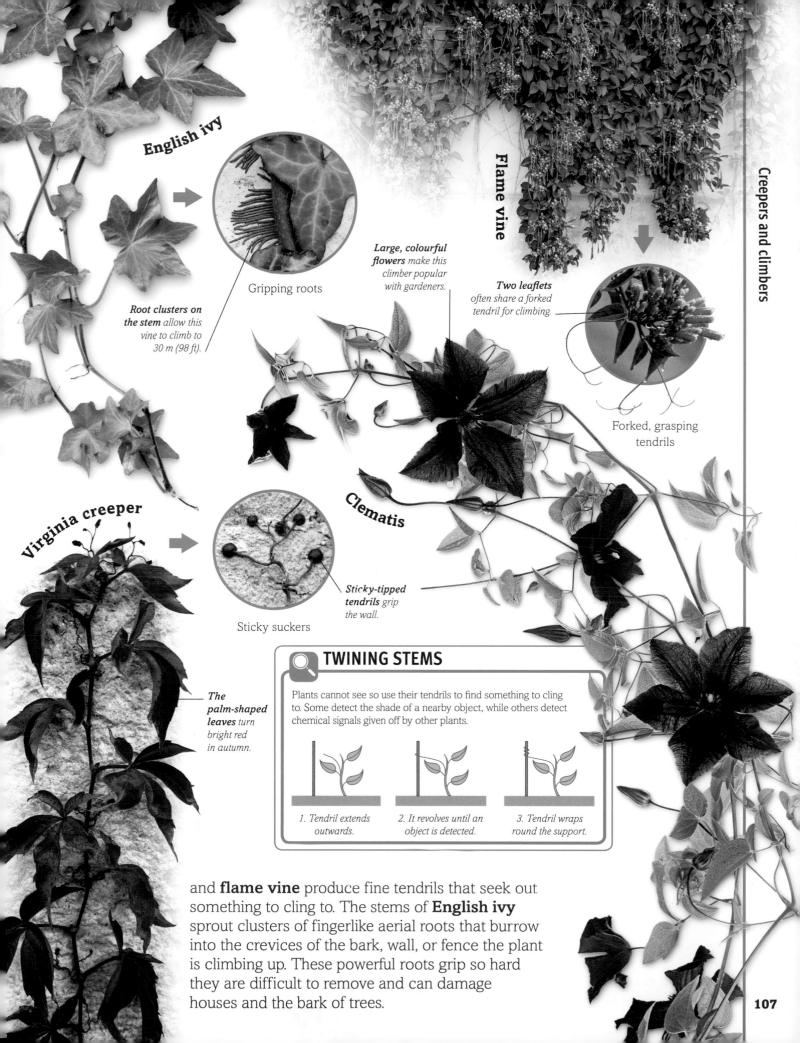

English ivy

Gripping roots

Root clusters on the stem allow this vine to climb to 30 m (98 ft).

Flame vine

Large, colourful flowers make this climber popular with gardeners.

Two leaflets often share a forked tendril for climbing.

Forked, grasping tendrils

Clematis

Virginia creeper

Sticky suckers

Sticky-tipped tendrils grip the wall.

The palm-shaped leaves turn bright red in autumn.

🔍 TWINING STEMS

Plants cannot see so use their tendrils to find something to cling to. Some detect the shade of a nearby object, while others detect chemical signals given off by other plants.

1. Tendril extends outwards.

2. It revolves until an object is detected.

3. Tendril wraps round the support.

and **flame vine** produce fine tendrils that seek out something to cling to. The stems of **English ivy** sprout clusters of fingerlike aerial roots that burrow into the crevices of the bark, wall, or fence the plant is climbing up. These powerful roots grip so hard they are difficult to remove and can damage houses and the bark of trees.

107

Bursting buds ❯ Leaves and new stems sprout from buds that protect the soft, delicate tissue from winter frosts. The new growth makes the bud burst open.

Leaf is tightly folded inside the bud, but soon bursts out.

Bud scales are tough and weatherproof.

Norway maple

Spring
As the weather gets warmer in spring, leaves begin to sprout from buds on the branches. The green leaves use sunlight to make food for the tree to grow and produce flowers.

Summer
Long days of sunlight allow the tree to make lots of food, and the tree is thick with leaves and yellow flowers, which are cross-pollinated primarily by bees. When fertilized, the flowers will become fruits and seeds will form.

Through the seasons
A deciduous tree, such as this Norway maple, has a cycle of growth that follows the seasons.

What is a tree?

Of all the plants, trees are the biggest and live the longest. Instead of green stems they have woody trunks, which usually divide into many branches. The woody tissue is very strong, allowing some trees to grow to incredible heights of 100 m (330 ft) or more. A network of roots anchors the tree to the ground, and draws up water and nutrients from the soil.

Trunk rings

The tough outer bark protects the layer of growing plant tissue beneath it.

Wide, pale rings form in spring, while narrow dark rings form later in the year.

The heartwood at the centre is the oldest part of the tree.

Cross-section of a tree trunk

Every year, a tree's trunk grows broader as a layer of woody tissue is added beneath the bark. The tissue grows fastest in spring, making softer wood, and more slowly late in the year, making harder wood. This forms annual growth rings, which are revealed if the tree is cut down.

Types of forest

Where there is enough rainfall for trees to grow in large numbers, they can form dense forests. The type of forest depends on the nature of the trees, which is determined by the climate.

Rainforest
In wet climates with no winter frosts, trees grow all year round to create rainforests. These are mostly found around the tropics.

Coniferous
The forests that grow in cold northern climates are mostly made up of tough evergreen conifer trees, such as pines and spruces.

Deciduous
Regions with long summers and short winters have forests of deciduous trees. They lose their leaves in autumn, but grow new ones in spring.

Autumn
As the days get colder and shorter, the tree stops making food. The chlorophyll that makes the leaves green begins to break down and they change from green to red and gold, and fall from the tree.

Winter
In the cold winter months, the branches are bare and the tree lies dormant, preserving its energy and water until the following spring.

Deciduous or evergreen?

Leaves change from green to red.

Deciduous tree in autumn

Evergreen tree

There are two main types of tree. Deciduous trees lose their leaves in winter as they stop growing. In spring, they produce thin leaves that make food efficiently, so the tree grows fast in summer. Evergreen trees have tougher leaves that make food more slowly, but which stay on the tree all year long.

Types of tree

These tall trees can grow to 45 m (147 ft) in height.

Broad

Sugar maple

Tall, columnlike trees have small, egg-shaped cones.

Stiff evergreen leaves grow in clusters at the ends of branches.

Broad **Elder**

Circles of white elderflowers are used to flavour drinks.

Mediterranean cypress

Dragon's blood tree

Autumnal yellow leaves all fall within a few days of each other.

Spreading

The bark of a dragon's blood tree **"bleeds"** a **blood-red sap** when cut.

Columnar **Ginkgo** Broad

Trees come in all shapes and sizes, depending on the conditions they live in. Trees in leaf all year round, with old ones constantly replaced by new ones, are called evergreen. Trees that lose all their leaves for part of the year are called deciduous.

Most evergreen trees are conifers, non-flowering plants such as the **Mediterranean cypress** and **Nordmann fir**. However some flowering trees with tough leaves are evergreen too. The **eucalyptus**, for example, has tough leaves with an oily coating to keep in water, which hang

This long-lived tree can survive for more than 1,000 years.

Bright red berries provide winter food for birds.

Oak

Round

Holly

Conical

Coconut

Slow-growing branches only extend about 4 cm (1 ¹/₂ in) a year.

Divided leaves allow harsh coastal winds to whip through without breaking the tree.

Palm

Branched

Joshua tree

Each needlelike leaf on this tree is up to 3.5 cm (1 ¹/₄ in) long.

This umbrellalike tree can grow up to 10 m (33 ft) in height.

The toxic leaves of this tree are harmless to koalas and possums.

Mature trees can produce two crops of figs each year.

Round

Common fig

Spreading

Eucalyptus

Nordmann fir

Conical

vertically, reducing exposure to the Sun during the Australian summers. Palms, such as the **coconut**, that grow in wet, warm tropical climates are also evergreen. Deciduous trees shed their leaves for part of the year, when conditions are too hot, cold, or dry. The **common fig** loses its leaves to survive the dry season, while the **elder**, **ginkgo**, **sugar maple**, and **oak** grow in regions with mild summers, but lose their leaves to help them survive cold winters. While **holly** lives in the same climate as these trees, its leathery evergreen leaves are able to tolerate the frosty winter conditions.

111

Barking up the tree

The red-brown bark can be up to 30 cm (11 in) thick.

Fibrous
(Coast redwood)

The green inner bark turns blue, purple, and orange when exposed to the air.

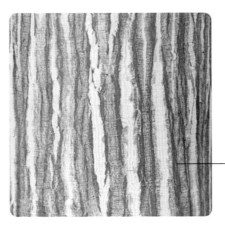

The bright green bark with white stripes is easily damaged in strong sunlight.

Vertical stripes
(Manchurian striped maple)

Spiny
(Silk floss)

Cone-shaped spines protect this greenish grey bark against animals.

Unusual rectangular plates make it easy to identify a persimmon tree's bark.

Plates
(Persimmon)

This smooth grey bark can be infected by deadly fungi.

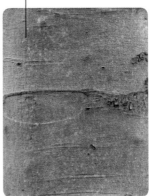

Smooth
(American beech)

Bark is the woody "skin" that protects the trunks of trees and stems of shrubs, forming a barrier against disease and grazing animals, while keeping water in. Bark is essentially dead tissue – a tough layer formed as the living cells underneath it die and are replaced.

Tree bark comes in many different patterns and textures and is vital to the health of a tree. The fibrous bark of the **coast redwood** is extremely fire-resistant, while the spines on **silk floss** bark deter any hungry animals from eating the young branches. As all trunks need air to

Mottled
(American sycamore)

Blotchy bark flakes off in large chunks.

Diamond-shaped pores join each other to form channels in older trees.

Diamond lenticels
(White poplar)

Oak bark contains tannins, which are chemicals used in making leather.

Horizontally broken ridges (Oak)

Flaking
(Pine)

In some
Aboriginal Australian
stories, ghost gums
are **living spirits**.

Deep cracks develop in the bark as the tree ages.

Rough lenticels break up the shiny, coppery brown bark.

Intersecting ridges
(Crack willow)

Horizontal lenticels
(Tibetan cherry)

Thick outer bark peels off to reveal soft inner bark.

Powdery, white bark reflects the heat of the strong Australian sun.

White
(Ghost gum)

Peeling strips (Rainbow eucalyptus)

survive, trees such as **white poplar** and **Tibetan cherry** develop spongy cracks called lenticels in their bark to let air pass through. Some bark naturally splits as the tree grows, revealing the inner layer beneath. This produces beautiful patterns on the **Manchurian striped maple**, the **Rainbow eucalyptus**, and the **American sycamore**. Trees can die if their bark is severely damaged. Mountain pine beetles can introduce a fungus under the bark of a **pine** tree to weaken it, allowing their eggs to hatch and the larvae to eat the living layer under the bark. The pine tree releases sticky resin to defend itself against these insects.

STANDING TALL North America's Pacific Coast is densely forested, with millions of conifer trees growing in the cool, wet conditions on the west side of the Rocky Mountains. Massive trees thrive in this climate, such as this old-growth redwood in California's Bear Creek Watershed. In the distance is Rockefeller Forest, the world's oldest continuous old-growth redwood forest, measuring more than 40 sq km (15 sq miles).

This tree may seem huge compared to its surroundings, but the title for the world's tallest tree goes to Hyperion, which stands at 116 m (380 ft) – or about twice the height of the Statue of Liberty in New York City, USA. The exact whereabouts of Hyperion, a coastal redwood, remains a closely guarded secret and there are no confirmed photographs of it. However, we do know it lies somewhere in northern California's Cascade Range, a part of the Redwood National Park, which also houses Helios and Icarus, the second and third tallest trees. Despite its great height, the 600–800-year-old Hyperion was not found until 2006, because it grows in a valley that hides its height from clear view.

Blossom time

Laburnum

Showers of yellow flowers give this tree its other name, "golden rain".

Pink flowers grow in clusters in spring, and produce purple seed pods.

This upright petal guides pollinators to the nectar.

Chinese redbud

Mock orange

The fragrant flowers of this tree contain oils used in perfumes.

These beautiful flowering branches spread out and provide shade in hot, tropical environments.

Royal poinciana

NATURAL DYE

In 2018, scientists created a natural dye using the bright red flowers of the royal poinciana tree. This dye can be used to colour silk and cotton fabrics.

Blossom is the name for the flowers that grow on trees and bushes, which often produce colourful displays in spring and summer. Changes in temperature and day length signal to the plant when to bloom. When pollinated, blossoms grow into fruits.

Some trees, such as **blackthorn** and **magnolia**, begin to flower even before their leaves unfurl, which may help pollinators find their flowers more easily. After pollination, fruits such as **mock oranges** and **apples**, as well as seed pods of trees such as **laburnum**

A healthy apple tree can produce fruits for more than 100 years.

Apple

These delicate pink and white blossoms produce fruit in autumn.

Each bud opens into a five-petalled flower in early spring.

Chinese fringetree

These feathery, snow-white flowers are mildy fragrant.

Blackthorn

Magnolia

Thick petals help flowers withstand pollination by big, clumsy beetles.

The blue flowers are produced for up to two months.

Jacaranda

Magnolia flowers have **bloomed** since the time of the **dinosaurs**.

and **Chinese redbud**, can take many months to develop. Although people usually grow flowering trees for their attractive flowers or edible fruit, some blossoms, such as those of magnolia, are also used in perfumes and traditional Chinese medicine. In Japan, festivals are held in early spring to celebrate the beauty of blossoming trees, particularly cherry and plum, with people coming from around the world to view the magnificent displays.

117

Living on air

Bristly moss produces spores that can grow into new moss plants.

Orthotrichum moss

These stiff leaves are specially adapted to absorb moisture from the air.

Tillandsia air plant

The undivided fronds grow up to 150 cm (59 in) in length.

Staghorn fern

Silvery leaves hang in chains.

Bird's nest fern

Spanish moss

Dense cushions of this moss grow in shady, damp areas.

Fissidens moss

Forked fronds like a deer's antlers give this plant its name.

Not all plants grow in soil. Some, known as epiphytes, anchor themselves onto other plants or tree trunks instead. These plants do not take nutrients from their hosts, however, they absorb water and nutrients from the air and rain, or sometimes from the dead leaves that collect around their base.

Mosses such as **fissidens moss** or **orthotrichum moss** can often be seen growing on walls or tree trunks. These tiny plants survive by storing water like a sponge. They then use this water to make food. **Spanish moss** is not really a moss at all, but a flowering plant. It is one of about

Necklace orchid

Waterproof leaves come in many colours and collect pools of water at their centre.

Long strings of flowers have a sweet scent to attract insect pollinators.

Frogs, insects, and even crabs can be found living in bromeliad pools.

Bromeliad

These yellow flowers resemble the golden gowns of dancing ladies, giving this orchid its name.

LIVING LAYERS

Rainforests are divided into four layers, each with its own unique set of plants and animals. Fungi living on the dark forest floor break down plant matter. Shrubs and bushes in the under canopy shelter small animals and predators in the shadow of a full, leafy canopy, which is home to birds and climbing animals. Emergent trees tower above all others, housing high-fliers such as eagles and bats.

Emergent layer

Canopy

Under canopy

Forest floor

Male **bees** attack the orchid, mistaking it for a rival, and **pollinating** it as they do so.

Dancing lady orchid

Long strap fern

The strap-shaped fronds grow up to 1 m (3 ft) long.

Leaves are covered with a waxy layer to reduce evaporation.

650 plants known as air plants. They take their name from their ability to use their leaves to absorb water from the air around them. Many epiphytic **orchids** grow in humid environments such as rainforests. They collect moisture from the air too, but use fleshy roots to do this, rather than their leaves. The **staghorn fern** also uses its roots to take in water from its humid environment, producing fronds that lie flat against the tree trunk to prevent them drying out. The crowns of fronds at the top of this plant and other epiphytic ferns, such as the **bird's nest fern** and the **long strap fern**, also collect water and falling leaves, which provide much-needed nutrients for these plants.

STRANGLER FIG

In Wat Mahathat, a Buddhist monastery in Ayutthaya, Thailand, a strangler fig wraps around the head of a broken Buddha statue. This type of fig starts life as a small seed dropped on a tree branch by an animal, such as a bird.

After germinating, the seedling's roots grow down the trunk of the tree, absorbing nutrients from soil deposits on the branches. Once they reach the ground, they burrow into the soil, helping the strangler fig to develop faster and send its shoots stretching higher for sunlight. Many roots wrap around the host tree, enclosing its trunk in a network that thickens and tightens as it grows, sometimes even killing the tree. Strangler figs will grow over anything that gets in their way, including walls and entire houses.

The forest floor

In temperate forests, plant life has to adapt to the four seasons. Flowers must shoot up early in the spring, before the trees start growing leaves, blocking the sunlight. Then plants that have evolved to live in the shade take over, such as ferns and mosses, surviving on the little light that filters through.

Bell-shaped flowers carpet forest floors in western Europe in spring.

Bluebells

These star-shaped flowers have a musky smell.

Calypso orchid

Wood anemone

Flower stems are held above the leaves to attract pollinators.

Cushions of moss can reach 10 cm (4 in) in height.

Hosta

Broom forkmoss

The hairs attract insects for pollination, but this orchid does not produce nutritious nectar.

These edible leaves have a garlicky smell and flavour.

Lady's slipper orchid

The pouch-shaped petals force insects to brush past the yellow pollen above, aiding pollination.

Wild garlic

The **wood anemone** is one of the first flowers to emerge in early spring. **Bluebells** and **wild garlic** soon follow, shooting up from underground bulbs and soaking up sunlight with their long leaves before the trees above burst into leaf. These plants are known as "spring ephemerals" because they spend just a few weeks in bloom before dying back, ready for next spring. The **white**

wakerobin survives like this for up to 70 years. Enclosed by a thick green canopy of leaves, the forest floor is dark, cool, and damp throughout the summer, ideal conditions for **sword ferns** and **mosses** to grow. In autumn the leaves fall from the trees, insulating the earth in the colder months, and building up a thick layer of matter to enrich the soil.

Each pinna (leaflet) has a lobe that sticks up at its base, giving it the shape of a sword hilt.

Sword fern

Six tepals grow around the anthers. The tepals curl back towards the stalk to advertise the flower to pollinators.

White wakerobin

A striped bract surrounds and covers each flower spike.

Fawn lily

This plant is **poisonous** but if cooked properly its root can be made into **bread**.

The three-petalled flowers first appear when this plant is 7–10 years old.

Jack-in-the-pulpit

Dense clumps grow slowly but can reach 1 m (3 ft) wide. Each leaf is no more than 9 mm (⅓ in) long.

Pincushion moss

Bonsai

Each miniature apple is up to 1 cm (²/₅ in) across, about one-fifth the size of a regular crab apple.

The **smallest bonsai** grows just **5 cm** (2 in) tall.

Dense growth on top makes this a favourite among bonsai lovers.

Scots pine

Satsuki azalea

Bright red berries cover female trees throughout the winter.

Japanese winterberry

Crab apple

This 18th-century Japanese print shows women examining a plant seller's bonsai.

Bonsai seller

Showers of purple flowers make wisteria a popular bonsai vine.

Wisteria

These funnel-shaped flowers can range from under 2 cm (⁴/₅ in) to 17 cm (6³/₄ in) across.

The word "bonsai" means "planted in a container" and is the Asian art of growing miniature trees. The small pot helps to restrict growth, while the branches are skilfully pruned to keep the plant small, and mimic the natural shape of the full-size tree.

Although they usually only reach a height of between 13–25 cm (5–10 in), bonsai trees bear flowers and fruit. Some species, such as the **wisteria** and **satsuki azalea**, are particularly popular for their beautiful displays of flowers, while others, including **crab apples** and **dwarf pomegranates**, produce tiny fruits. Bonsai

PRUNING A BONSAI

Special scissors are used to trim bonsai branches in order to make an attractive tree shape, while preventing the trees from growing too quickly.

Chinese juniper

Dramatic shapes are created by pruning or twisting branches around wires, which are later removed.

Autumn leaves make a colourful display popular with bonsai enthusiasts.

Japanese maple

Dwarf pomegranate

Pink, white, red, or purple blossoms usually bloom in May, which is called "satsuki" in Japanese – giving this tree its name.

Chinese elm

Rocks are often used to create dramatic bonsai designs.

The branches and trunk of this bonsai have been trained to give it a windswept look.

requires careful pruning of the shoots and roots, and it takes skill not to kill the trees in the process. The **Chinese elm** bonsai is more likely to survive mistakes made by beginners. One **Chinese juniper** in Japan has been proven to be about 1,000 years old, with centuries of careful pruning and shaping by bonsai masters. With enough time and care, a bonsai tree can become extremely valuable. The most expensive bonsai ever sold was in 2011. It had a price tag of 100,000,000 Japanese yen, equivalent to around £840,000 ($1.3 million).

What is a grass?

Grasses are short plants with long, narrow leaves, jointed stems, and flowers that are almost always arranged in spikes. This group of plants first appeared on land more than 66 million years ago, evolving over time into the 12,000 species of grass today. Grasses cover huge areas of land on every continent, and are more widely spread than any other type of plant.

Grass flowers

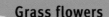

Meadow foxtail flower

Anthers poke out of the flowers and bob in the wind, releasing pollen grains.

Grasses produce flower spikes with many small flowers, which are wind-pollinated. As they mature, each flower dangles its anthers in the wind, allowing millions of pollen grains to be blown away to fertilize the feathery, sticky stigmas of another grass. Since grasses do not have to attract animal pollinators, their flowers have lost their colourful petals.

Growing point > Grasses can survive continual grazing by wild and farm animals because their growing point is at the base of their stem, close to the soil. When nibbling animals eat the leaves, they leave this growing point intact, allowing the plant to regrow easily.

Leaf blade ❯ Many grasses have long, thin leaves with parallel veins running down the length of each blade. Each new leaf emerges from within the base of the older blade.

Sweet vernal grass

Leaf sheaths grow at the base of each grass leaf. Wrapped around the stem, leaf sheaths prevent stems from breaking and also protect the growing point.

Roots ❯ Grasses have very dense root systems that hold the plant in place even when being tugged at by large grazing animals. These root clusters also hold the soil together, preventing erosion.

Grass imposters

Rush
This snowy woodrush has long, thin leaves that may look like those of a grass, but it is actually a rush, and belongs to a related family of plants.

Seagrass
These seagrasses live on the ocean floor, providing an important habitat and food source for a wide range of fish and other marine life.

Sedge
Sedges are wetland plants with grasslike leaves, but you can tell them apart from grasses and rushes by their triangular stems.

Grasslands

Grassland habitats cover about a third of all land on Earth. They are found in regions too dry to support a forest but too wet to be a desert. From African savannas to North American prairies to European meadows, grasslands support a huge variety of wildlife around the world, such as the Grant's gazelles seen here. Wildfires often sweep across grasslands, encouraging thick grass regrowth and removing tree seedlings.

Types of grass

When you think of grass, you might picture a garden lawn, but there are thousands of very different species, including crops such as rice, and even bamboo. They may not be the most colourful plants, but they are some of the most important. Grasses grow in habitats around the world, including deserts, mountains, and rainforests.

Ornamental bamboo

The blue-grey leaves grow in clumps up to 20 cm (7 ¾ in) in height.

Blue fescue

Antarctic hair grass

This tiny grass is one of two flowering plants native to Antarctica.

Grasslands make up around **one-third** of all land on Earth.

Divided flower stems look like a crow's foot, giving this grass its name.

Grasslike leaves grow from woody stems, unlike other grasses.

Crowfoot grass

Although most grasses look similar, some have unique features that make them stand out. While **bamboos** grow woody stems that allow some species to reach up to 50 m (160 ft) in height, the **Antarctic hair grass** lives in such a harsh, cold climate that it grows only a few centimetres tall. Most grasses come in shades of green but some are popular for their colours, such as the red leaves of the **Japanese bloodgrass** and the blue-grey foliage of the **blue fescue**. The red flower spikes of the **hair-awn muhly grass** add a splash of colour to gardens, while many people grow **pampas grass** for their tall, feathery flower spikes, which blow in the wind.

These fluffy flower tufts are popular with gardeners.

Hares-tail grass

TALL AND USEFUL

Elephant grass can grow into a tall plant quickly, without needing much water or food. Thriving even in poor soil conditions, African elephant grass is used as fodder for cattle and elephants. It is also planted to prevent soil erosion in dry or overgrazed lands. Scientists have explored the use of the Asian variety of this grass as a biofuel, burning it to produce electricity.

4 m (13 ft)

The flattened flower spikes are just 1 cm (¹/₃ in) long.

Spangle grass

Flower spikes look like fluffy pink clouds.

Hair-awn muhly grass

Soft flower spikes look like grey bottle brushes.

Japanese bloodgrass

Oriental fountain grass

This tall grass can reach 3 m (9¾ in) in height.

Pampas grass

Blood-red leaf tips fade to bright green at the bottom.

Grasses and grains

Grasses produce the grains that feed the world. Grasses with edible seeds or grains are known as cereal plants, and have been cultivated for thousands of years. Today, cereals are harvested on a massive scale across the world.

Sugarcane

Oats are usually crushed and made into porridge.

Grains of rice

When ready to harvest, sugarcane can be twice the height of a grown man.

Rice

This wetland plant is grown in watery fields called paddies.

The sweet sap extracted from this stem is dried to make cane sugar.

Oat grains

Oat

Drought-tolerant cereals are an important source of food in Africa.

Ears of wheat hold up to 80 grains each.

Sorghum grains

Sorghum

Wheat

Crystals of sugar

Wheat grains

The most widely grown cereal plant is **maize**. Maize kernels are mainly used as cattle feed, or turned into a liquid biofuel called ethanol. Next comes **rice**, an essential food crop for more than half the people on the planet, especially in Asia. **Wheat**, the third most important grain, is usually ground into flour and used to make bread and pasta. **Barley**, which comes fourth, is used both for food and to make alcoholic drinks. Fifth is **sugarcane**, a large grass grown for its sweet sap, which is extracted by crushing the stems. The syrupy liquid is evaporated until it is so concentrated it will harden when cooled, and the resulting solid is ground up into sugar crystals.

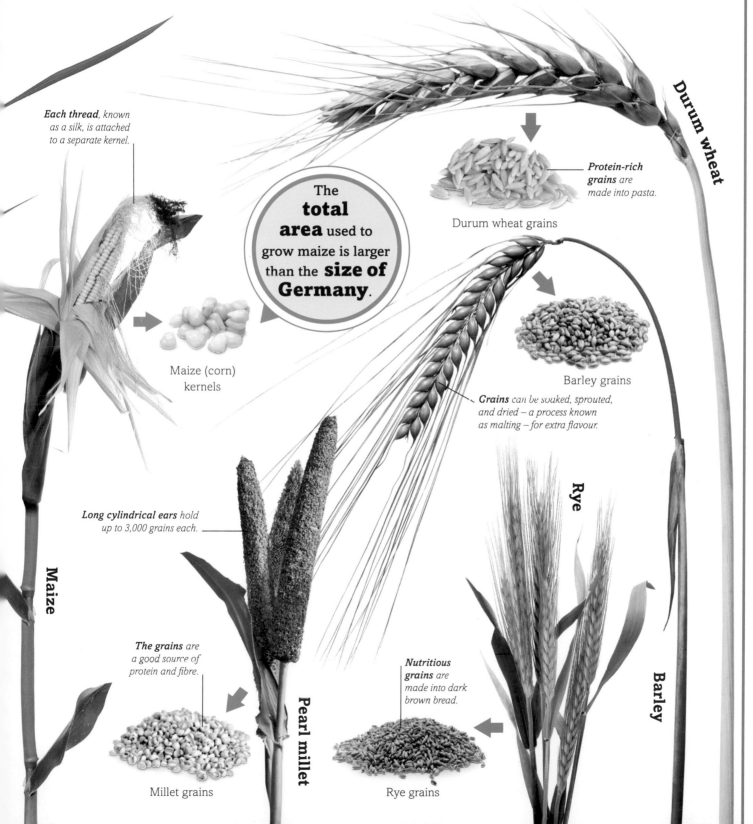

Each thread, known as a silk, is attached to a separate kernel.

Protein-rich grains are made into pasta.

Durum wheat grains

Durum wheat

The **total area** used to grow maize is larger than the **size of Germany**.

Maize (corn) kernels

Barley grains

Grains can be soaked, sprouted, and dried – a process known as malting – for extra flavour.

Rye

Maize

Long cylindrical ears hold up to 3,000 grains each.

Barley

The grains are a good source of protein and fibre.

Pearl millet

Nutritious grains are made into dark brown bread.

Millet grains

Rye grains

131

RICE TERRACES
A rice farmer working on these spectacular, lush-green fields needs a good head for heights. The precisely stepped staircases, which rise almost vertically in some parts, are located about 280 km (174 miles) from Vietnam's capital city, Hanoi. One of the world's most widely consumed foods, rice is grown all over southeast Asia and is hugely important to the economy of many countries.

These layered rice fields in the Mu Cang Chai district of northeastern Vietnam were carved out of the mountainsides hundreds of years ago. With simple handtools, early farmers laboured to make use of every scrap of fertile land. Today, the terraces produce much of the country's rice. Covering about 2,000 hectares (4,900 acres), the plants change colour from green to gold with the seasons. Growing rice is still hard work, even today. It is difficult to use machinery on such a steep incline so work is done by hand. After planting, farmers are constantly weeding, and in the run up to harvest, the terraces are kept flooded with streamwater carried by farmers down the mountains in bamboo pipes.

What is a fruit?

A fruit develops from a plant's fertilized flower. It encloses and protects the seeds while they develop, then helps to spread them. The sweet flesh of most fruits encourages animals – including humans – to eat them, spreading their seeds in the process.

Tasty bananas come ready-wrapped in a tough protective skin.

Banana

Kiwi

Strawberry

A ripe strawberry is bright red, and packed with vitamins and nutrients.

Seed ❯ Most fleshy fruits, such as this kiwi, develop as a tasty package to hold the seeds. Fleshy fruits often change colour as they ripen, so that animals can spot and eat them, dispersing their seeds.

Bananas are a type of berry, but most have been bred to not contain seeds.

What is a vegetable?

Vegetables are any edible part of a plant except for the fruit. We eat fleshy roots, succulent stems, flowers, buds, and leaves. Because all these parts of the plant are making or storing food, they are rich in vitamins, which make them good food for us.

Cabbage

Carrot

Root ❯ A root vegetable is the underground part of the plant. It can be the plant's food store in the winter, and contains starch, sugar, and vitamins. High in nutrients and fibre, edible roots are an important part of a healthy diet.

Leaf ❯ A leaf makes food, and so contains energy and minerals. The fibre in leaves that makes them sturdy helps human digestion.

Pear

Apple

Brown pear seeds are found in a central core, within the fleshy fruit.

Fig

Figs are eaten fresh and dried.

The thin red peel forms an attractive layer around the flesh, to attract animals.

Fruit or vegetable?

Any part of a plant we eat is either a fruit or a vegetable. Fruits develop from fertilized flowers, and contain seeds that are spread when they are eaten. Any edible part of the plant that is not a fruit is a vegetable. This can be a root, a stem, a leaf, or even the buds of developing flowers.

Asparagus

Stem ❯ A stem transports food to and from the roots of a plant, and is full of minerals. When stems are soft enough, they can be eaten as vegetables, raw or cooked.

False fruits and vegetables

We often use the terms "fruit" and "vegetable", based on how we eat plants – in sweet or savoury dishes – rather than how they grow. So, a sweet-tasting vegetable is sometimes called a fruit, while a savoury salad fruit may be called a vegetable!

Rhubarb is an example of a false fruit. It is actually a stem vegetable.

A tomato is an example of a false vegetable. It is actually a fruit.

Going underground

These underground stems grow at the bottom of ponds.

Arrowhead

Dandelion

Beetroot

Parsnip

This plant's bitter roots are used to treat many illnesses.

The white root turns purple when exposed to sunlight.

Turnip

The red juice from beetroot is used as a natural food colouring.

COLOSSAL CARROT

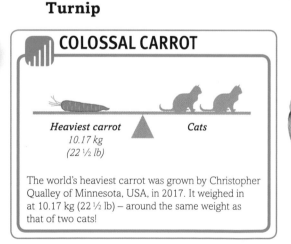

Heaviest carrot
10.17 kg
(22 ½ lb)

Cats

The world's heaviest carrot was grown by Christopher Qualley of Minnesota, USA, in 2017. It weighed in at 10.17 kg (22 ½ lb) – around the same weight as that of two cats!

This root becomes sweeter after winter frosts.

Air channels form a distinctive pattern.

Lotus root

Vegetables that grow underground can be stored for long periods of time, making them important food crops, especially when other foods are scarce. The swollen roots store energy, which the plants use to regrow in the spring – if they are not eaten first!

Many underground vegetables, including **parsnip**, **beetroot**, **carrot**, **swede**, and **daikon**, are made of swollen roots, but others store energy in different ways. **Arrowhead** and **taro** plants store energy in bulblike stems called corms, while **lotus roots** are modified stems that grow

Taro

Swede

This large root can grow up to 30 cm (12 in) long, and is eaten as a winter food by people and cattle.

Radish

This underground stem is an important food in tropical regions of Africa and Asia.

Colourful varieties are grown for their high vitamin content.

Potato

These peppery roots are eaten raw in salads

Carrot

Cassava

This tropical root is used to produce flour and can also be eaten as a vegetable.

The knobbly tubers become sweeter when left in the Sun.

Daikon

Long white roots grow up to 60 cm (23½ in) long and are a popular food in Asia.

Oca

These crunchy roots taste sweet and come in a variety of colours.

horizontally, called rhizomes. **Potatoes** and **ocas** are tubers made from swollen stems, and have spots called eyes from which new shoots can grow. Many root vegetables are vital food sources. **Cassava**, for example, can be grown in poor, dry soils, and is a staple food in many parts of Africa. The **dandelion** is perhaps best known for its yellow flowers, but its roots can be used to make tea, which is believed to have medicinal properties.

Soft fruits

Goji berry

Ripening fruits change colour from white to red to purple.

These oval berries have a sweet-sour taste and are eaten dried.

Blackcurrant

Redcurrant

Up to 25 red berries are produced on each stem.

Mulberry

Raspberry

The fruits are delicious fresh or in a jam.

This is a cluster of "drupelets" – mini fruits each with a seed inside.

The dark purple berries are used to make jams and syrups.

Cloudberry

Cranberry sauce is traditionally eaten with turkey on Christmas.

Blackberry

This hardy plant can survive extreme cold.

Lingonberry

Cranberry

These amber-coloured fruits are rich in vitamin C.

The juicy, thin-skinned fruits we call berries, with pulpy flesh and seeds rather than a stone, are also known as soft fruits. Most are sweet, some are sour, but all are rich in vitamins. Wild berries have been an important source of food for thousands of years.

Most soft fruits grow on bushes and shrubs, but **mulberries**, **Yangmei fruits**, and **goji berries** grow on trees. **Cranberry** bushes are unusual because they grow in bogs. These are flooded before harvest, and special machines called eggbeaters are sent in to knock the cranberries from the

Vine leaves are edible, too, wrapped around savoury fillings.

Each Yangmei tree can produce up to 100 kg (220 lb) of fruit in one summer.

Clusters of fruits can contain up to 300 grapes.

Grapes have been grown for **making wine** for more than **8,000 years**.

Grapes

Yangmei fruits

Dark blue berries grow up to 1.6 cm (¹/₂ in) across.

Blueberry

Yellow seeds are actually tiny fruits on a sweet, swollen stem.

Strawberry

plants so they float away and can be skimmed from the surface of the water. In Scandinavia, **cloudberries** and **lingonberries** are mostly picked from wild bushes. **Grapes** hang in bunches from long vines and come in several different colours, from green to black. They are eaten fresh, made into wine, and dried to make raisins and currants. **Strawberries** ripen on small, low-growing plants. The big, fat, juicy fruits we eat today have been cultivated from tiny, but delicious, wild strawberries the size of peas.

VOLCANIC VINEYARD
Centuries ago, erupting volcanoes smothered the Spanish island of Lanzarote in ash, ending traditional farming but creating a unique environment for grapevines. Although it may not look it, the volcanic ash in the wine-making region of La Geria is very fertile. This nutrition-rich soil combined with warm days and cold nights make this an ideal region for growing grapes.

There is not much rain on Lanzarote, but in La Geria's vineyards, an ingenious method of cultivating vines ensures that every available drop of moisture reaches the growing plants. Each young vine is placed in a shallow individual pit. Any rainfall or overnight dew is channelled down the sloping walls of the pit to reach the roots of the vine nestling at the bottom. The low, surrounding semi-circular stone walls protect the vines from the wind and help to prevent the ground from drying out. This technique has been used successfully for many years. Around 10,000 vines grow in the La Geria valley, producing red and white wines. The area is recognized as a Protected Landscape.

Stone fruits

Cherry

These red fruits usually grow in pairs on a single, short stem.

Plum

Dried, shrivelled plums are known as prunes.

Olive

Hard and bitter, olives are processed before eating, or pressed for their oil.

Peach

Fuzzy skin protects the easily bruised flesh of this fruit.

Green and unripe, this fruit tastes like an apple, but then turns purple and sweet like a date.

Jujube

The large, round seed makes up 80 per cent of the berry's interior.

Acai berry

This flat, oval seed can grow up to 7 cm (2¾ in) long, and is tricky to cut out.

Mango

The green, unripe fruit can be eaten before the almond inside hardens.

Almond

These thin-skinned, firm, often fleshy fruits, with a single, hard seed at the centre, are known as drupes or, more commonly, stone fruits. Many have been cultivated from wild trees to produce bigger, juicier fruits.

The sweet fruits of the hardy **date palm** have been a vital source of food for desert peoples for thousands of years. Delicious fresh, they can also be dried and stored for long periods of time. The sweet, juicy flesh of **peaches** is delicious when eaten fresh, though some people don't like its

Sloe

These small, slightly sour fruits are used to make preserves and flavour spirits.

Dates

Nectarine

The hard, wrinkled stone protects an almond-shaped seed.

Date palms can produce up to **140 kg** (310 lb) of fruit each year.

These high-growing fruits are picked with the help of ropes, ladders, or cherry-picker trucks.

This fragrant fruit is eaten both fresh and dried.

The pulp of this bitter fruit is used to make jams.

Apricot

Damson

fuzzy skin, and prefer its smooth-skinned relative, the **nectarine**. Some stone fruits are not sweet but sour – the **sloe** must be cooked up with lots of sugar. The flesh of **olives** is hard as well as bitter. But when crushed in a press, a greenish gold oil can be extracted. Some stone fruits, such as **almonds**, are grown for their edible seeds, rather than their flesh. Some people do eat whole unripe green almonds, which are fuzzy, crunchy, and tart, with a soft, jelly-filled seed.

Juicy fruits

Pomelo

The pale flesh tastes like a sweet grapefruit.

Buddha's hand

This finger-shaped fruit smells like a mix of lemon and lavender.

Blood orange

The bright red flesh gives this orange its name.

Orange

A regular-sized orange contains about one-third of a cup of juice.

Citrus fruits are a type of berry with a pulpy, juicy flesh, covered by a thick peel. They are widely eaten because of their tangy flavours and are rich in vitamins. Originally from Asia, citrus fruits are now grown in tropical countries around the world.

Scientists believe that the dozens of citrus fruits available today can be traced back to just three ancestral plants, the **pomelo**, the mandarin orange, and the **citron**. Today, **oranges** make up more than 50 per cent of all citrus fruits produced worldwide. Their sharp, tangy

Lemon

Citron

The bright green peel turns yellow as the fruit ripens.

The yellow outer layer, which is full of flavour, is called the zest.

Key lime

The thick peel is used to make jams.

Kumquat

These bite-sized fruits do not require peeling.

Kaffir lime

Jamaican tangelo

A tangelo's skin is loose and easy to peel.

The thick, white inner layer is called the pith.

These knobbly fruits are used to make citrus-scented perfumes.

The large fruits can grow up to 15 cm (5 in) across.

Grapefruit

flavour comes from the high content of citric acid, which is highest in **lemons** and **limes**. Unlike most citrus fruits, the **Buddha's hand** has little edible flesh, and is instead used in perfumes and as an offering in Buddhist temples. The peel of most citrus fruits is tough and bitter, while the segments inside are juicy. The exception to this rule is the **kumquat**, which has a sweet peel and a bitter centre. The **Jamaican tangelo** is a natural mix of an orange and a pomelo, with very juicy, sweet-tasting flesh and a wrinkled, fragrant peel.

Tropical fruits

The spiky skin protects tangy yellow flesh.

Pineapple

Each fruit contains around 250 edible seeds.

Passion fruit

This star-shaped fruit comes in sweet and sour varieties.

Star fruit

The world's largest tree-borne fruit, it can grow up to 90 cm (36 in) long.

Jackfruit

This sweet fruit is usually eaten like an apple.

Persimmon

The long, soft spines turn red or yellow when the fruit is ripe.

Sweet, fleshy fruit contains spicy-tasting seeds that can be used as a substitute for pepper.

This giant fruit, packed full of smaller fruits inside, can weigh up to 55 kg (121 lb).

Papaya

Tropical fruits come in a wide range of shapes, sizes, and flavours. These colourful fruits grow in warm, wet regions, but are now shipped all over the world where they have become very popular.

While all the tropical fruits shown here are commonly eaten raw and whole, many are also used in a range of other ways. **Pineapples** and **passion fruits** are often juiced, while **rambutans** and **guavas** are made into jams. The white fruits inside **jackfruits** can be used

Speckled flesh tastes faintly of kiwi fruit.

Rambutan

Inside the fruit

Dragon fruit

Hairy, brittle skin encloses edible white flesh inside.

Chikoo

The juicy flesh has a grainy texture and tastes like caramel.

Vivid pink flesh tastes like a mix of pear and strawberry.

Durian

Guava

Cream-coloured flesh tastes like sweet custard with a hint of onion.

White segments are sweet and tangy.

Inedible skin

Mangosteen

Lychee

This perfumed fruit encases a large, oval-shaped seed.

in baking, and their stringy texture has made them popular as an alternative to meat in vegetarian and vegan cooking. Asian dishes are sometimes sweetened using **star fruits** and **papayas**. **Persimmons** are used to add flavour to smoothies and cold desserts, while **lychees** are poached in syrup to be eaten with ice creams. The smelly **durian** has a unique flavour that some love and others hate. Known as the king of fruits, durians are used to make a huge variety of sweet treats, including candies, cakes, and ice cream.

Magnificent melons

Large, flat-bottomed, with a sweet, slightly spicy flavour, some consider this the king of melons!

Crenshaw melon

Nicknamed "little mouse watermelon", this grape-sized Mexican fruit tastes like a cucumber.

Cucamelon

These striped fruits are small enough to fit in the palm of your hand.

Tigger melon

The flesh of a watermelon is a thirst-quenching 92 per cent water!

Watermelon

Gac

When ripe, this melon has spiny red skin, yellow flesh, and slimy red seeds.

This rare Indian melon has fragrant flesh and stripes like a beachball.

Kajari melon

Melons are the sweeter relatives of cucumbers, gourds, and pumpkins, and they come in all shapes, sizes, tastes, and colours. There are hundreds of varieties, but they all grow best where the climate is warm and there is plenty of water.

These juicy fruits originally came from Africa and the Middle East, but are enjoyed all over the world today. They grow on vines, have a tough skin, and there are two main types – sweet melons and watermelons. Sweet melons include **honeydew, charentais,**

HYDROPONIC MELONS

Hydroponics is a method of growing plants indoors in a liquid full of nutrients. It can produce more food than crops grown in soil because of the controlled environment, in which temperature, light, and humidity can be regulated. This is a good method for growing melons, which need a lot of water.

Bitter melon

Warty, unripe fruits are used in many Asian dishes.

The orange flesh is a good source of vitamins.

Charentais melon

Yubari King melon

Considered a rare treat, just two of these fruits sold for £21,500 ($28,000) in Japan in 2016.

Sweet, pale green flesh is enclosed within a thick, waxy rind.

Honeydew melon

Jellylike flesh tastes like a cross between a banana and a cucumber.

This thin-skinned fruit can be eaten whole – rind and all.

Korean melon

Santa Claus melon

This melon takes its name from the fact that it keeps well, almost until Christmas!

Horned melon

Kajari, Korean, tigger, Santa Claus, Yubari King and most of the other melons shown above. Even the odd-looking **horned melon**, an important source of food and water in the Kalahari Desert of Namibia, and the prickly **gac** from southeast Asia, are related.

The most commonly grown melon is the **watermelon**. It's also the heaviest. An average specimen is about 10 kg (22 lb), but the biggest ever recorded weighed in at 159 kg (350 lb) – that's equal to the weight of an adult male panda!

A bit nutty

Almond
These edible seeds are packed with fibre, protein, and healthy fats.

Hazelnuts

Turkish hazelnut
Frilly husk covers all but the tip of the nut.

Macadamia
The shells of these large nuts are the hardest among all nuts.

Pistachio
The shell changes colour from green to beige as the seed ripens, opening with a pop.

Walnut
The two halves of the wrinkly fruit are separated by a partition.

Coconut
Hollow seeds are creamy white with a clear liquid inside.

TRUE VS FALSE NUT

A true nut is a hardened fruit containing one seed. False nuts develop inside fruits, and are more like the core of an apple.

This shell is a fruit's fleshy body that happens to be hard.

This is a seed and not the entire fruit.

Acorn (true nut)

Brazil nuts (false nut)

True nuts, such as chestnuts, acorns, and hazelnuts, are hard fruits containing a seed. Many of the nuts we eat are actually the seeds of fruits, or false nuts. To avoid confusion between the two, all edible nuts are called culinary nuts.

Nuts have been eaten by humans for thousands of years. Their high fat and protein contents make them a nutritious food. They do not rot or perish quickly, so early humans could store them for the winter months. Many culinary nuts are the seeds of fleshy stone fruits similar

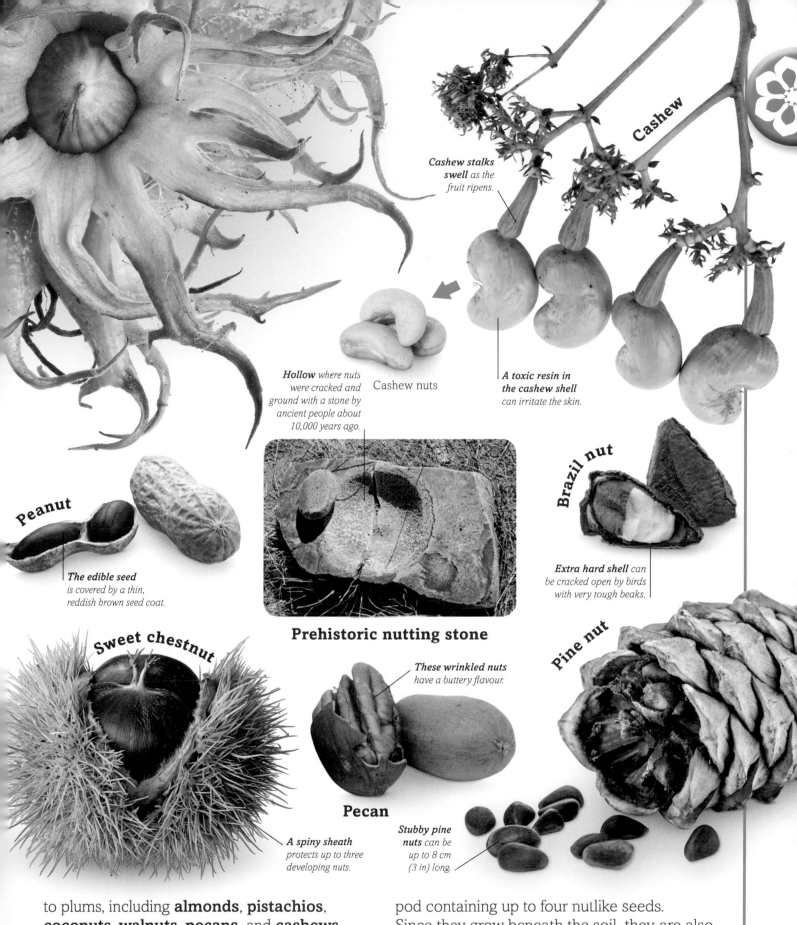

Cashew stalks swell as the fruit ripens.

Cashew

Hollow where nuts were cracked and ground with a stone by ancient people about 10,000 years ago.

Cashew nuts

A toxic resin in the cashew shell can irritate the skin.

Brazil nut

Peanut

The edible seed is covered by a thin, reddish brown seed coat.

Prehistoric nutting stone

Extra hard shell can be cracked open by birds with very tough beaks.

Pine nut

Sweet chestnut

These wrinkled nuts have a buttery flavour.

Pecan

A spiny sheath protects up to three developing nuts.

Stubby pine nuts can be up to 8 cm (3 in) long.

to plums, including **almonds**, **pistachios**, **coconuts**, **walnuts**, **pecans**, and **cashews**, while **pine nuts** are seeds found inside pine cones. **Peanuts** are the strangest so-called nut. Once pollinated, peanut flowers push a stalk into the soil to produce an underground bean pod containing up to four nutlike seeds. Since they grow beneath the soil, they are also known as groundnuts. Of the nuts shown here, **hazelnuts** and **sweet chestnuts** are the only "true" nuts. Their hard shells are the flesh of the fruit, while the part we eat is the seed.

Eat your greens!

Savoy cabbage

These fibrous, wrinkly leaves keep their shape when cooked.

Lettuce

Raw leaves are often added to salads.

The red leaves give this plant its other name, red chicory.

Radicchio

Peppery leaf adds a spicy flavour to salads.

Rainbow chard

Brussels sprouts

Rocket

Leafy greens contain **vitamin K**, which helps **wounds heal**.

Small, round leaf buds resemble baby cabbages.

These colourful plants are packed with vitamin K and other essential nutrients.

Almost 2,500 plants are known to have leaves you can eat, but some taste better than others. While many leafy vegetables are eaten raw in salads, others are cooked into a wide variety of dishes around the world. Packed with nutrients, these edible leaves come in many colours and shapes, and form an essential part of a healthy diet.

Kale

The bitter leaves become sweeter after a frost.

Bok choy

The crunchy leaf stalks can be eaten raw or stir-fried.

Red cabbage

The leaves of the red cabbage are sweeter and tougher than those of the white cabbage.

Tightly packed ball of leaves

Spinach

These delicate leaves lose water and shrivel up when cooked.

Watercress

These peppery leaves grow both on land and in streams.

Endive

Inner leaves are pale because they receive less sunlight.

GIANT CABBAGE

Heaviest cabbage
(62.7 kg / 138 1/3 lb)

Children
(Weight of two children)

The heaviest cabbage ever grown was a whopping 62.7 kg (138 1/3 lb), the average weight of two young children. It was grown in Alaska, USA, in 2012.

For thousands of years, people have cultivated leafy vegetables to produce new varieties that give better harvests and more interesting flavours. The results of these gradual changes can be clearly seen in the differences between vegetables like **brussels sprouts, savoy cabbage, kale, red cabbage**, and broccoli all of which are the same species of plant.

Each was bred by humans for bigger leaves, more leaf buds, thicker leaf stalks, or different colours. The vibrant **rainbow chard** and **radicchio** plants seen today are also a result of careful selection by breeders over time. The crisp **lettuce**, too, was once a weed with prickly leaves and stems, and was grown by the ancient Egyptians for its oily seeds.

Peas and beans

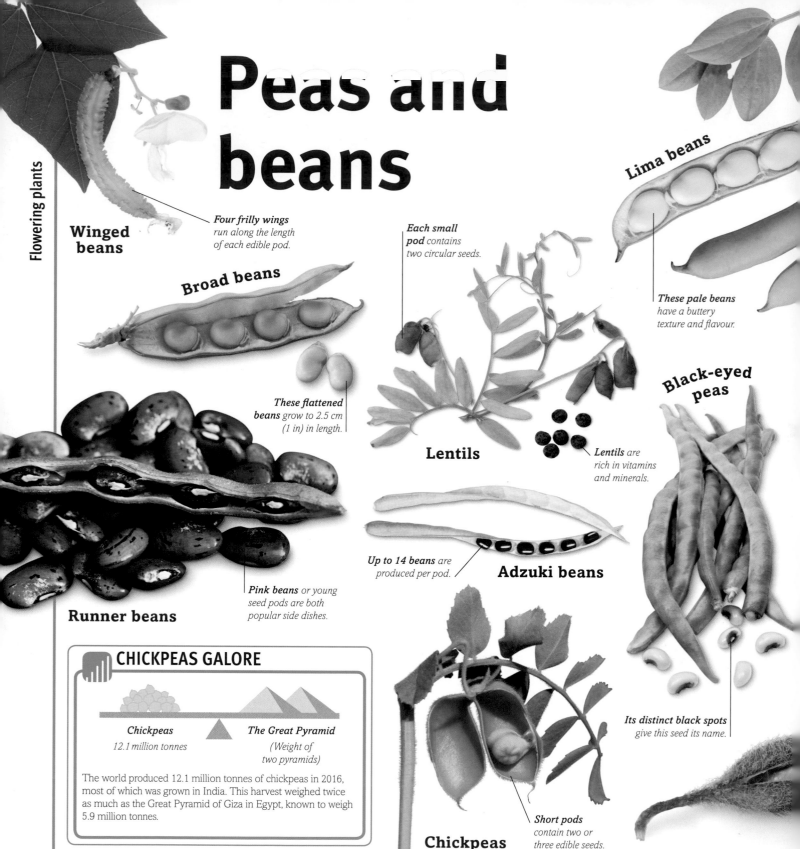

Winged beans

Four frilly wings run along the length of each edible pod.

Broad beans

These flattened beans grow to 2.5 cm (1 in) in length.

Lima beans

These pale beans have a buttery texture and flavour.

Each small pod contains two circular seeds.

Lentils

Lentils are rich in vitamins and minerals.

Black-eyed peas

Runner beans

Pink beans or young seed pods are both popular side dishes.

Up to 14 beans are produced per pod.

Adzuki beans

Its distinct black spots give this seed its name.

CHICKPEAS GALORE

Chickpeas
12.1 million tonnes

The Great Pyramid
(Weight of two pyramids)

The world produced 12.1 million tonnes of chickpeas in 2016, most of which was grown in India. This harvest weighed twice as much as the Great Pyramid of Giza in Egypt, known to weigh 5.9 million tonnes.

Chickpeas

Short pods contain two or three edible seeds.

Peas, beans, and lentils are types of seed known as pulses. They are rich in proteins, fibre, and nutrients, and have been eaten by humans around the world for thousands of years. Today, India is the biggest grower and consumer of pulses, particularly lentils.

Humans started farming pulses because their seeds can be easily dried and stored for when food is scarce. **Lentils** are one of our oldest crops, with archaeological evidence showing that humans ate them more than 13,000 years ago in Greece, while 7,500-year-old **chickpeas** have been found in excavations in Turkey.

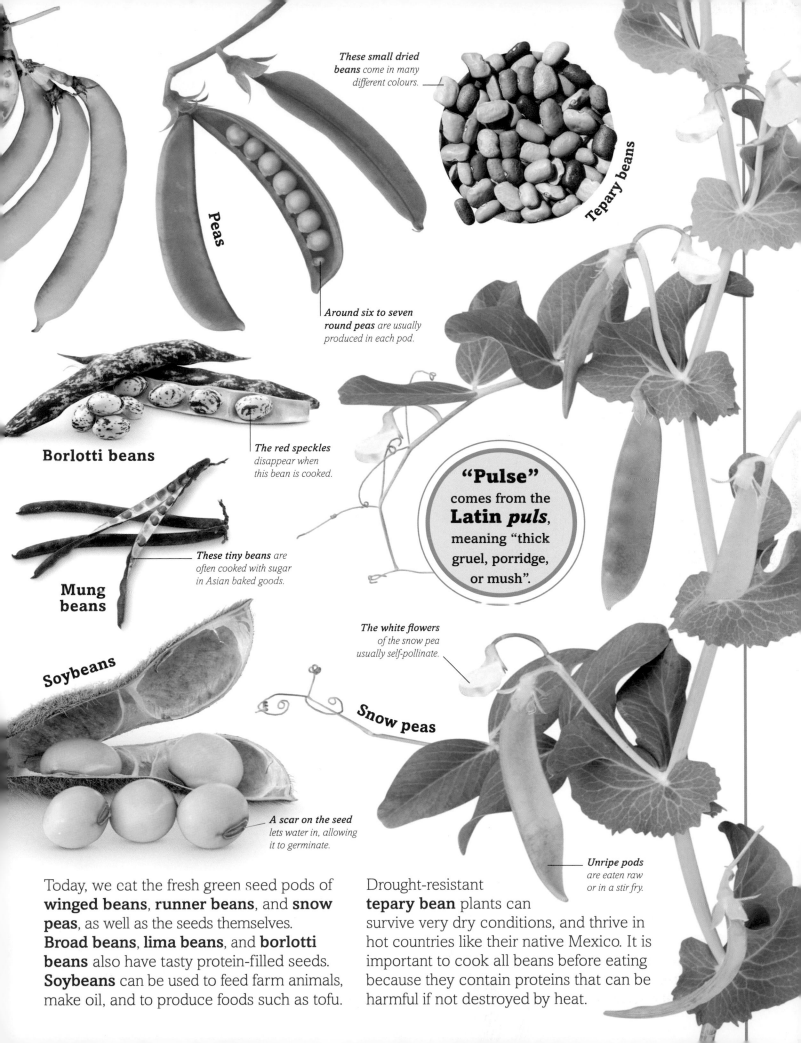

These small dried **beans** _come in many different colours._

Peas

Tepary beans

Around six to seven **round peas** _are usually produced in each pod._

Borlotti beans

The red speckles disappear when this bean is cooked.

"Pulse" comes from the **Latin _puls_**, meaning "thick gruel, porridge, or mush".

These tiny beans are often cooked with sugar in Asian baked goods.

Mung beans

The white flowers of the snow pea usually self-pollinate.

Soybeans

Snow peas

A scar on the seed lets water in, allowing it to germinate.

Unripe pods are eaten raw or in a stir fry.

Today, we eat the fresh green seed pods of **winged beans**, **runner beans**, and **snow peas**, as well as the seeds themselves. **Broad beans**, **lima beans**, and **borlotti beans** also have tasty protein-filled seeds. **Soybeans** can be used to feed farm animals, make oil, and to produce foods such as tofu.

Drought-resistant **tepary bean** plants can survive very dry conditions, and thrive in hot countries like their native Mexico. It is important to cook all beans before eating because they contain proteins that can be harmful if not destroyed by heat.

All squashed up!

This stripy squash can grow up to 50 cm (19½ in) long.

Green pumpkin

Edible seeds, held inside bright yellow flesh, are a good source of zinc.

Cushaw pumpkin

A hooked neck gives this warty yellow squash its name.

Crookneck squashes

The round fruits change colour from green to orange as they ripen.

Pumpkin

PLUMP PUMPKIN

Heaviest pumpkin 1,190.49 kg (2,624¾ lb)

Hatchback car

The world record for the heaviest pumpkin ever grown was in 2016 for a fruit weighing 1,190.49 kg (2,624¾ lb), around the same weight as a hatchback car.

Although they are typically eaten as vegetables, squashes are actually the fruits of creeping vine plants that belong to the gourd family. There are many types of squash and they come in lots of curious shapes.

Almost all species of squash originally come from Central and South America, but are now grown around the world, particularly in India and China. These large and fleshy fruits are rich in vitamins. The vitamin content is particularly high in squashes with orange and yellow flesh, such

The fibrous skeleton of a dried and peeled luffa can be used with soap and water as a bath sponge.

Dried luffa

This fruit's skin turns bitter once the luffa grows longer than 10–12 cm (4–4¾ in).

The teardrop-shaped fruits taste like chestnuts and are popular in Japan.

Red kuri squash

The green skin is a great source of fibre.

Cucumber

Luffa

Thick necks do not contain seeds, so yield a lot of flesh.

These giant squashes can weigh up to 18 kg (39½ lb), but are much tastier when smaller.

Butternut squash

Blue Hubbard squash

Hulusi flutes are traditional Chinese instruments made of a gourd and three bamboo pipes.

Long necks can stretch to more than 90 cm (35 in).

Gourd

Tromboncino

Shaped like a flying saucer, these fruits are a slightly sweeter version of a courgette.

Pattypan squashes

as **green pumpkins** and **red kuri squashes**. Most of these fruits are cooked and eaten as savoury dishes such as soups and stews, but some sweeter varieties, including **pumpkin** and **butternut squash**, are also baked into cakes and pies. **Cucumbers** are typically eaten raw or pickled. Edible **pattypan squashes** are popular autumnal decorations, while other squashes with hard skins, known as **gourds**, can be dried and used to make everyday items such as jars, bottles, or even musical instruments, including maracas, flutes, and drums.

PUMPKIN BOAT RACE
Paddling giant pumpkins for canoes, contestants race round a lake at the Tualatin Pumpkin Regatta in Oregon, USA. Held every autumn, such events are hugely popular not just in the United States, but also in countries including Canada and Germany. Pumpkins are easily converted into boats, as they are already partly hollow inside, making it a simple task to carve out space for a rower to sit inside.

Developing from star-shaped, yellow flowers, the bigger varieties of pumpkins can swell rapidly to enormous sizes – some measure more than 4 m (13 ft) round the middle and weigh 450 kg (992 lb). In the Tualatin race, competitors wearing fancy dress and lifejackets paddle their pumpkins 90 m (295 ft) and back. Pumpkins are also the main attraction in a variety of other holidays and festivals. American families gather every year for Thanksgiving, which is famous for its pumpkin pie. At Halloween, on 31 October each year, children in many countries carve out pumpkins to look like scary or funny faces, then put a candle inside to give them an eerie glow, to frighten off evil spirits.

Bulbs, stems, and stalks

Onion

When cut, these fleshy bulbs release a chemical that makes your eyes sting and water.

Bark is stripped from the trunk to reveal the crunchy vegetable inside.

Harvesting palm trunks

Heart of palm

Cardoon

Leaf stalks are eaten after removing the spiny leaf blades.

Celeriac

The thick stem tastes like celery and can reach up to 15 cm (6 in) across.

Rhubarb

Fleshy leaf stalks are often stewed with sugar and eaten in desserts.

Asparagus

Leek

Spears of asparagus emerge from the earth in spring.

OVERSIZED ONION

In 2014, the largest ever onion was grown in the UK. The ginormous bulb weighed 8.5 kg (18¾ lb), approximately the same weight as a pug dog.

Largest onion   *Pug*

The cylindrical bulbs turn white underground.

Many plants make food in the warmer months and then store it in their bulbs, stems, and stalks. This makes these vegetables a valuable food source for the winter months, and people have eaten them for thousands of years.

Bulbs, such as **leeks**, **onions**, and **garlic**, are made up of fleshy leaves, while **celeriac**, **asparagus**, and **kohlrabi** are swollen stems that are tastiest eaten when young and tender. Other vegetables,

Kohlrabi

Swollen stems taste like a sweeter version of broccoli.

Garlic

Up to 20 cloves of garlic make up each bulb.

The feathery leaves, swollen stem, and seeds all taste like liquorice.

Water chestnuts are **grown underwater** in flooded fields called **paddies**.

Water chestnut

The crunchy underground stem is often eaten in Chinese dishes.

Bamboo shoot

These conical, tender shoots of the bamboo plant are widely used in Asian cooking.

The salty stems of this coastal plant are often eaten with fish.

Samphire

Fennel

including **rhubarb** and **cardoons**, are the leaf stalks of the plant, although the leaves themselves are not edible. The enlarged base of **fennel** is made of both swollen stems and leaf stalks. The growing tips of many different types of **bamboo** are eaten as bamboo shoots, but harvesting them does not harm the mature plant.

However, young bamboo shoots contain natural toxins, which must be removed by boiling in water. **Hearts of palm** are harvested from the trunks of several types of palm tree. **Samphire** is an asparagus-like plant that grows in coastal areas. Its stems can be eaten raw or boiled.

LIVING WITH PLANTS

Plants and people

The earliest people were hunter-gatherers, always on the move searching for food such as meat, berries, and seeds. Then around 12,000 years ago, the first farming began in the Fertile Crescent, a region in the Middle East. Here people settled down and learned to sow, harvest, and store crops – the ancestors of wild grasses – and domesticate animals.

How plants have changed

Humans have cultivated many plants since farming began. An ancient wild relative of maize, called teosinte, bore just a few hard kernels. Farmers noticed that some teosinte plants produced more kernels and with a softer texture, so planted these for the next season. Over time, this selective farming method led to the large cobs we eat today.

A hard coat makes the few kernels tough to eat.

Teosinte   **Maize**

Sowing seeds ❯ For thousands of years people have sowed seeds by hand. Here, as the man drives the plough, the woman follows behind sowing the seeds,

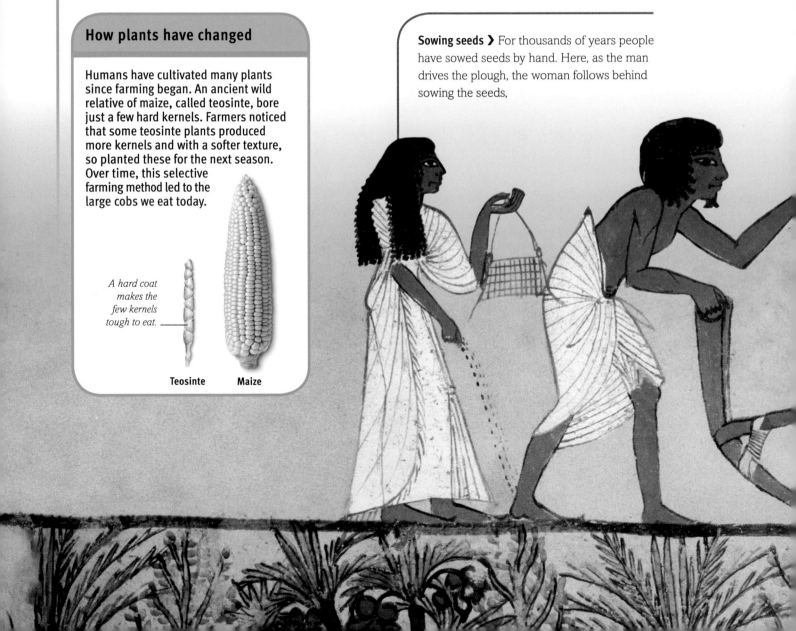

Modern farming methods

Not only have the plants we farm changed, modern agricultural machines help us to sow, grow, and harvest crops more easily and quickly than ever before. Over the centuries the population of the world has exploded, and continues to grow. Without modern farming methods billions of people would go hungry.

To harvest a field using a machine, the entire crop must mature at the same speed and reach a similar height.

Combine harvester

Farming in ancient Egypt

In ancient Egypt, farming began along the banks of the River Nile. Every summer the river flooded the land, leaving fields watered and rich in nutrients. Here the ancient Egyptians grew staple foods, such as wheat and barley, as well as a variety of fruits and vegetables.

Other ways people use plants

Medicine
From headaches to cancer, more than 50,000 plants around the world are used to treat diseases.

Cosmetics
Many plant-based chemicals that are fragrant or moisturising are used in cosmetics such as shampoos and perfumes.

Furniture
Trees provide all the timber used to make furniture. Forests must be carefully managed to replace the trees that are used.

Paper
Most paper comes from trees. Wood chips are mixed with water to make a pulp, which is flattened and dried into thin sheets.

Building materials
Timber is also a popular building material for houses because it is strong, insulating, and environmentally friendly.

Clothes
The seed fibres of cotton and stem fibres of flax, hemp, and bamboo are often used to make fabrics.

Musical instruments
The woods of some trees can produce deep, rich sounds, and have been used for centuries to make musical instruments.

Cattle-drawn plough > The first ploughs were pulled by people. The ancient Egyptians were the first to domesticate cattle and use them to pull heavier ploughs to cut tracks in the soil for sowing the seed.

The spices of life

The young, green berries *turn brown once dried in the Sun.*

Cumin

Dried seeds

Allspice

Dried berries

Each seed pod *releases a single cumin seed when dried.*

Turmeric

These seeds *have a nutty flavour, and are common in Asian and Middle Eastern cuisines.*

Dried seeds

Sesame

Wasabi

Fiery green wasabi sauce *is eaten with sushi in Japan.*

Paste

This red fruit *contains capsaicin, a chemical that gives chillies their spicy heat.*

Underground stems, or rhizomes, *are ground into bright yellow powder.*

Prairie fire chillies

Star anise

Dried fruits

The star-shaped fruit *tastes like liquorice.*

Fresh and dried turmeric

Without spices – the dried seeds, fruits, roots, and bark of plants – our food would be much less tasty. For thousands of years, people have been adding spices to their cooking to flavour, colour, and preserve their food. Some spices, such as turmeric and ginger, are used as health remedies, too.

Dried seeds

Cubelike seeds are often used in Indian cooking.

Fenugreek

These tiny black seeds are ground to make a hot sauce.

Dried seeds

Each droopy seed pod can grow up to 15 cm (6 in) in length.

Vanilla

Mustard

Dried seed pods

The inner bark of the cinnamon tree is harvested and cut into small sticks.

Harvesting cinnamon

Cinnamon sticks

Unripe fruits are cooked and dried into peppercorns.

Dried fruits

Black pepper

Peppercorns are the world's most **commonly traded** spice.

Each seed pod contains about a dozen cardamom seeds.

Dried seed pods

Green cardamom

The red, outer covering around this seed is used to make another spice called mace.

Dried seeds

Nutmeg

Ginger

Underground stems have a hot, spicy flavour.

The fragrant red stigmas are harvested carefully by hand.

Saffron

Many spices come from tropical plants from East Asia. Our appetite for their flavours makes them highly valuable, and it was the demand for spices that drove European explorers and traders to sail the globe in search of precious supplies in the 15th and 16th centuries. The Italian explorer Christopher Columbus reached the Caribbean Islands while trying to find a new spice trade route to India. Instead, he found **chilli** peppers, which he brought back to Europe. Today we take for granted the exotic ingredients in our kitchen cupboards. We can't imagine not having **pepper** on the table, a hot dog without **mustard**, or ice cream without **vanilla**. The most expensive spice in the world is **saffron**, which is worth more than gold by weight.

Helpful herbs

Flat-leaf parsley

Curly parsley

Chewing these leaves can help freshen breath after eating garlic.

Thyme

In German folklore, places where **thyme** grows wild are said to be **blessed** by fairies.

These fragrant leaves were once given to knights before battle to inspire courage.

Leaves have a strong taste and in ancient Greece and Rome were fed to chariot horses to give them strength.

MUMMIFICATION

In ancient Egypt, people who died were mummified to preserve their bodies. After cleaning and embalming the body of a dead person, it was wrapped in linen bandages, along with herbs such as thyme and mint. The herbs' fresh and fragrant scents were considered sacred.

The leaves are most well known as the dried herb used on pizza toppings.

Oregano

Coriander

The aromatic leaves have a tart, lemony flavour.

Herbs are plants that are used to flavour food, give perfume its smell, or provide medicinal qualities. Some have fragrant leaves or flowers that can be eaten fresh. Others are woody and added to cooking or used dried.

Using herbs dates back to ancient times. In ancient Greece, eating **thyme** was believed to cure poisoning, while **rosemary** was thought to help memory, and scholars used to put rosemary in their hair to help them during exams.

Spicy leaves *taste like liquorice and are used in Asian cooking.*

Thai basil

Dill

Dill seeds *are used as a spice.*

In the past, these hairy, grey-green leaves were used to ward off evil.

Mint

These delicate, feathery leaves *are often eaten with seafood.*

Dill leaves

These leaves *are used in toothpaste and sweets.*

Sage

Rosemary

Chives

The leaves *are used for flavouring food.*

Needlelike rosemary leaves *grow on woody plants that can reach up to 2 m (7 ft) tall.*

The hollow, tubular stems *taste like onion – and the flowers do too!*

In the Middle Ages, herb gardens were common in European monasteries: monks grew **sage** as a remedy and also to clean their teeth. The plant's scientific name, *Salvia*, comes from the Latin for "I am well". **Oregano** is also healing. In Chinese medicine, it is used to help digestive problems.

Modern science has proven some of the qualities of herbs – **mint** oil is known to kill mosquito larvae, for example. Other ideas are based on superstition, such as the medieval practice of drinking **dill** tea to repel a witch's curse.

Plant products

Plants provide many of the materials we use every day. From tree trunks we harvest timber to build houses, wood to turn into paper, and resins to make varnish. Dyes can be made from berries and leaves, and textiles from plant fibres. Some plants have many uses. In Malaysia, for example, the coconut palm is called the "tree of a thousand uses" because almost every part of this tree is useful.

Fruit ❯ The large, smooth fruits of the coconut palm contain a seed known as the coconut. It has a hard, hairy shell and edible white flesh.

Coconut water, the liquid found inside the immature seed, is a delicious drink that is rich in nutrients.

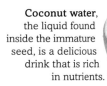

Utensils, such as this cup, can be carved from coconut shells.

Ropes can be made from coir, the fibres of the coconut husk.

Oil is extracted from the white flesh for use in cooking.

Musical instruments, such as this Hawaiian pahu drum, are made from coconut timber.

Logs of coconut timber are often used in construction because they do not decay easily.

Trunk ❯ Coconut palms can grow up to 30 m (98 ½ ft) tall. Their slender, flexible trunks, which have a ringed pattern, allow them to bend rather than break in strong winds.

A male flower opens, sheds pollen, and falls off within a day.

Sugar is made from the sweet sap in the stalks of the flower buds.

Flower ❯ Coconut flower spikes contain stalks growing from a fleshy stem. Male flowers grow at the top of these stalks, while female ones grow at their base. Both types of flower produce nectar to attract insects.

Coconut palm

Brooms are made from the stiff, dried midribs of coconut leaves.

Coconut leaves can grow up to 1.8 m (6 ft) wide.

Baskets can be made by weaving together the leaflets of coconut leaves.

Leaf ❯ Mature coconut palms have around 35 leaves, each of which grows from a single bud at the top of the tree. Coconut leaves can grow up to 6 m (19¾ ft) in length.

Other plants and their products

Cotton
White fibres surround the seeds of the cotton plant. In the wild, these fibres drift off in the wind, carrying the seeds to new places to grow. The fibres can be removed from the seeds and spun into threads to make textiles.

Thread

Hemp
This was one of the first plants to be used for clothing. The long fibres that make up the stem of the plant are used to make threads that can be woven into fabrics or twisted into string.

String

Cork oak
The waterproof outer bark of the cork oak tree is used to make stoppers for bottles, floor tiles, and many other household objects. The bark grows slowly and is harvested once a decade.

Cork stopper

Layer of bark has been removed.

Rubber
The milky sap of the rubber tree is harvested by cutting a line into its trunk and collecting the liquid that drips out. When set, rubber is an elastic material used to make gloves, shoe soles, and tyres.

Tyre

SHRINKING FOREST
Mist rises in the hot air above a mountain rainforest known as the Leuser Ecosystem, on the Indonesian island of Sumatra. Dense with trees pushing up through the rainforest layers, the tallest rise 45–60 m (150–200 ft), to emerge above the canopy. This unique habitat is the last place where Sumatran orangutans, tigers, elephants, and rhinoceroses co-exist in the wild.

Tropical rainforests cover around 6 per cent of the world's land, yet produce 40 per cent of all oxygen, and are often called the lungs of Earth. The Leuser Ecosystem covers around 26,300 sq km (10,100 sq miles), about the size of the US state of Massachusetts. However, rainforest cover in Indonesia is rapidly decreasing to make room for palm oil plantations, hydroelectric dams, and farming. Increase in demand for timber and wood pulp for paper has led to a rise in illegal logging. Human activity is putting many of the species of plants and animals in the region, which are not found anywhere else in the world, at risk of extinction. It also threatens the health of the whole planet.

Natural beauty

Henna leaves are crushed before they can be used as hair dye or to decorate hands and feet for special occasions.

Henna

Hand decorated with henna

This scented paste is made from powdered sandalwood, and is used as a skin cleanser.

Sandalwood

Perfume

Cucumber extract has soothing properties and is used widely in skincare products.

The yellow-gold oil is, in fact, a liquid wax made from seeds.

Jojoba

Waxy yellow flowers have an exotic fragrance.

Cucumber

For thousands of years, people have used plant products to make themselves look and smell good. Floral fragrances and plant-based potions are still big business today, with many people preferring to use natural products rather than artificial ones.

Many different parts of plants are used to make beauty products. **Ylang-ylang** and **lavender** flowers each contain scents that can be distilled for use in perfumes. **Sandalwood** is just that – the aromatic, oily inner wood of a tree, which has natural antiseptic and healing qualities.

174

Nut butter

Fatty seeds are used to make shea butter, a popular moisturiser.

Shea

Lavender

Dried flowers are used to extract oil.

Cocoa

The fragrant oil has soothing, healing qualities.

Goats climb argan trees to eat the fruit, and **disperse** the **seeds** in their droppings.

Argan

Cocoa butter, made from the crushed insides of cocoa beans, is melted to make body creams.

Dried cocoa beans

This thick, fleshy leaf has a gel-like sap inside.

Oil extracted from the seed nourishes skin, hair, and nails.

Clear leaf sap is added to many skin care products for its soothing properties.

Body scrub mixed with argan oil

Inside an aloe vera leaf

Bath bombs infused with eucalyptus oil nourish hair and soothe the skin.

Aloe vera

Eucalyptus bath bombs

Eucalyptus

While the seeds of the **shea** nut, kernels of the **argan** fruit, and **cocoa** beans must all be roasted in order to release their rich oils, the seeds of the **jojoba** plant can simply be crushed. It is the leaves of the **henna** plant which, when dried and mashed to a paste, release a strong orange-brown dye. The sap inside the thick spiky leaves of the **aloe vera** plant is not only a soothing gel for burns, but has moisturising properties, too. Cleopatra, the queen of ancient Egypt, attributed her great beauty to her use of aloe vera!

Plants of the world

Australian postage stamps have featured its national flower – the fluffy golden wattle.

Golden wattle
Australia

Cattleya orchid
Brazil

This 100 yen coin shows cherry blossoms that are celebrated in Japan each year in the spring festival hanami.

Cherry blossom Japan

The blue of this national flower is used on Estonia's flag to represent the country's sea, sky, and lakes.

These huge flowers can grow up to 20 cm (8 in) across.

Cornflower
Estonia

This wildflower from Bhutan has distinctive yellow or amber anthers.

Himalayan blue poppy
Bhutan

This colourful flower, also known as the flame lily, belongs to a plant that is protected in Zimbabwe.

Coffee plant
Ethiopia

The arabica coffee plant originates in Ethiopia.

The maple leaf associated with Canada symbolizes unity, peace, and tolerance.

Rose mallow South Korea

This is a wreath of Pakistan's national flower, the sweet-smelling jasmine.

Glory lily Zimbabwe

Maple
Canada

This flower is also known as mugunghwa, which means "eternal blossom that never fades".

Jasmine Pakistan

Countries around the world often have a special connection to particular plants, rare or common. Many use flowers or trees as national symbols, often because these plants are culturally or spiritually important to the people living there.

Some countries choose a beautiful local flower to represent their nation, such as the showy **cattleya orchids** of Brazil and the **glory lily** of Zimbabwe. Australia observes Wattle Day on 1 September to celebrate the **golden wattle** that grows

According to a legend, tea was first made from tea leaves in China in 2737 BCE.

Tea China

The bell-shaped flowers of this Chilean vine bloom between March and May.

CORREOS DE CHILE
15 CTS
CASA DE MONEDA DE CHILE

Chilean bellflower Chile

Iris France

This flower inspired the fleur-de-lis symbol, used by the kings of France.

The rose was a symbol of royalty in England and later became the national flower.

Rose England

The cone-shaped centre holds the growing seeds.

Purple lavender flowers grow on spikes and appear across Portugal in the summer.

Lavender Portugal

In Portugal, **lavender** was believed to **ward off** evil spirits.

The lotus is the sacred symbol of India, and represents purity and grace.

Lotus India

across southern Australia as a sign of spring. The national flower of Bhutan, the **Himalayan blue poppy**, is so rare that it was once believed to be a myth, and is called the "blue yeti". The national tree of Canada, the syrup-producing **maple** tree, is found in each of its provinces, and its leaf features on the Canadian flag. The country that comes to mind when you say "tea" is China, the first to brew the hot drink from the plant's leaves – and the world's biggest producer today. In India, the national flower is the **lotus**. Hindu gods are often shown standing on this sacred flower.

Plant science

Although people have always relied on plants, the science of plants – known as botany – has only been studied for around 2,500 years. Early scientists described the medicinal properties of plants, while later researchers investigated them to learn how they survive and thrive.

350 BCE

Theophrastus, a student of the Greek philosopher Aristotle, is the first to study plants for their own sake. He writes the first botanical books, describing around 500 plants.

THEOPHRASTE

1200s

Arabian scientist Ibn al-Baytār writes the *Compendium on Simple Medicaments and Foods*, featuring the names of 1,400 plants, foods, drugs, and their uses.

1600s

Hydroponics, a method of growing plants in a nutrient-filled liquid rather than in the soil, is first described in the 1600s. This technique can produce more food in the same space, and is a popular method of growing plants today.

Ibn al-Baytār was one of the most influential writers on botany in medieval times.

60 CE

Greek botanist Pedanius Dioscorides writes *De Materia Medica*, a book on medicinal plants, which is used for the next 1,500 years.

The garden exists today in its original location, in Padua, Italy.

1545

The world's oldest botanical garden, the *Orto Botanico di Padova*, is built. The garden was used to grow medicinal plants, and teach students about them.

1561

The plant *Cordia sebestena* is named after German botanist Valerius Cordus. He describes plant features and medicinal properties for the first time in his book *Historia Plantarum*, published in 1561.

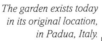

1789

English naturalist Gilbert White describes the time of year that different plants bloom. Today, scientists use this information to study how climate change is affecting flowering times.

Most plastics will not break down for thousands of years, but plant-based "bioplastics" have been developed that will break down into compost.

Every kernel on one ear of corn is unique and can look different from one another.

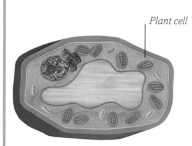

1800s

Austrian monk and scientist Gregor Mendel uses pea plants to explore how plants inherit their characteristics. Like humans, a plant gets half of its characteristics from the female plant and half from the male plant.

1838

German botanist Matthias Jakob Schleiden publishes *Contributions to Phytogenesis*, in which he argues that all plants are made of tiny units called cells.

Plant cell

1983

American scientist Barbara McClintock is awarded the Nobel Prize in 1983 for her research into the inheritance of maize (corn) traits and how this is controlled. This work has led to other important discoveries in the field of genetics.

2008

The Svalbard Global Seed Bank is built in Norway in 2008. This building stores seeds from around the world in case they are needed in the future.

1753

Swedish botanist Carl Linnaeus publishes *Species Plantarum*, which establishes the scientific naming system for plant organisms.

1950s

American scientist Norman Borlaug develops a disease-resistant, dwarf wheat variety, which helps feed billions. Before the 1950s, tall wheat plants often blew over before the top-heavy crops could be harvested.

The book contains data on the 5,940 plants known at the time.

SPACE GARDEN
Over millions of years of evolution, plants have become perfectly adapted for life on Earth. They are most certainly not adapted to growing in space, yet that is exactly what the plants shown here are doing. As part of an experiment on the International Space Station (ISS), its crew members are growing fresh vegetables in a "space garden" to try and improve their diet.

Plants are sensitive to their surroundings. Their roots grow towards sources of water, and their stems grow towards the light. They also react to gravity, growing up and away from its downward pull. In space, however, these plants are growing in zero gravity, with their roots held down by woven mats. The attraction of the artificial lights above them makes them grow upright, like plants on Earth. They are given water containing vital nutrients, and the ISS crew breathes out the carbon dioxide the plants use to make the sugar they need to grow. In this process, the plants give off oxygen, which improves the air quality within the space station, while the sugar is turned into plant tissue that the crew can eat.

Glossary

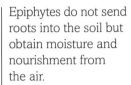

Aerial root
A root that grows from the stem of a plant above the surface of the ground.

Algae
Plantlike, mostly water-dwelling, organisms such as seaweed, which contain the green pigment chlorophyll.

Anther
The part of the flower's stamen that produces pollen.

Bark
The tough outer layer of the roots, trunk, and branches of woody plants such as trees and shrubs.

Buttress root
A root that grows out from the trunk of a tree, giving it extra support.

Canopy
An almost continuous layer of branches and leaves formed high above the ground by tree tops.

Biofuel
A renewable fuel produced from plant matter, algae, or animal waste.

Bonsai
A tree or shrub grown in a pot and kept in miniature form by special pruning. Bonsai is also the name given to this type of pruning.

Bract
A specialized type of leaf. Bracts, sometimes brightly coloured, help to protect buds and flowers on some plants, and can also serve to attract pollinators.

Bulb
Underground fleshy leaves that store food for a plant.

Chlorophyll
A green pigment. Plants use the chlorophyll in their cells to harvest the energy in sunlight.

Compound leaf
A leaf that is divided into two or more leaflets.

Conifer
An evergreen tree or shrub that has needlelike leaves. All conifers bear cones.

Corm
A swollen, bulblike underground stem.

Cotyledon
The first food-storing leaf, or pair of leaves, formed inside a seed.

Deciduous
Describes a plant that sheds its leaves each year at the end of a growing season.

Dicot
A flowering plant that produces two seed leaves (cotyledons) when it first starts to grow.

Dormant
In an inactive state. Many plants become dormant in the winter or in times of drought, remaining alive but shutting down to save energy.

Drupe
A fleshy fruit, such as a plum or cherry, containing a single hard seed or stone.

Epiphyte
A plant that grows on another plant for support without taking nutrients from it.

Epiphytes do not send roots into the soil but obtain moisture and nourishment from the air.

Evergreen
A plant that keeps its leaves throughout the year.

Fertilization
The combination of a male cell from pollen and a female egg, which goes on to produce a young plant known as an embryo.

Floret
A small flower, usually one of many making up the head of a flower such as a daisy.

Frond
A long leaf that usually consists of smaller leaflets. They are seen in plants such as ferns and palms.

Fungus
Microorganisms including mushrooms and toadstools. Fungi are more closely related to animals than to plants.

Germination
The process in which a seed starts to sprout and grow into a plant.

Harvest
The process of cutting and gathering crops from the field when ripe.

Host plant
A plant that is used by another for support and/or nutrients.

Inflorescence
A group of flowers on a single stem.

Kernel
A grain or the inner part of a fruit, stone, or nut.

Lateral root
A root that extends sideways from a main root to anchor a plant more firmly in the soil.

Leaflet
One of the smaller leaflike parts of a compound leaf growing from the leaf stalk.

Lenticel
One of the tiny pores on a plant stem that helps in the exchange of gases between the plant and its environment.

Lichen
An organism made up of a fungus and an alga, working together.

Monocot
A flowering plant that produces just one seed leaf (cotyledon) when it starts to grow.

Nectar
The sugary liquid produced by plants to attract pollinating animals.

Node
A point on a stem from which leaves, shoots, branches, or flowers can grow.

Nutrients
Minerals used by a plant to fuel its growth.

Parasitic plant
A plant that lives on another and takes nutrients from it.

Petals
The brightly coloured parts of a flower that attract pollinating insects and birds to a plant.

Photosynthesis
The process by which a green plant uses the energy in sunlight to create food for itself from water in the soil and carbon dioxide in the air.

Plant
A living organism, from a moss to a tree, that produces its own food by photosynthesis.

Pneumatophore
A straight aerial root that extends upwards through swampy soil, enabling a plant to exchange gases, or "breathe".

Pollen
The tiny powdery grains that contain the male reproductive cells, which combine with the female reproductive cells of a plant to make seeds.

Pollination
The transfer of pollen grains from a male flower, or part of a flower, to the female parts of a flower, to fertilize the eggs so seeds can develop.

Pollinator
An animal, such as a bee, moth, or bird, that makes the fertilization of plants possible by moving pollen from flower to flower.

Rhizome
An underground stem that grows horizontally, putting out shoots and roots as it spreads.

Root hair
A microscopic hairlike growth that extends from a root and increases the amount of water and nutrients that a plant can take in.

Sap
The juices in plant cells.

Sepal
A small, leaflike flap, usually green, that surrounds and protects the petals of a flower.

Setting seed
The process in which a plant starts producing seeds after its flowers have been pollinated.

Spore
A tiny reproductive structure found in non-flowering plants such as ferns.

Stamen
The male part of a flower that includes the pollen-producing anther.

Stigma
The female part of a flower.

Succulent
A plant that stores water in thickened, fleshy leaves or stems. Succulents include cacti.

Taproot
A thick, central root that grows straight downwards.

Tendril
A threadlike, twining stalk that vine plants use to attach themselves to a supporting object.

Tuber
A thick underground stem or root that some plants use for storing nutrients.

Vine
A plant that climbs or trails along the ground, supporting its stem with tendrils or by twining itself round a supporting object.

Plant index

In this book, plants are called by their "common names" – the names used in everyday life by ordinary people, and which can vary from country to country. However, when scientists across the world talk about a plant, they use its scientific name to avoid confusion. This is based on an internationally recognized naming system and is in Latin. A plant's scientific name is made up of two parts: the first is the genus, or group, of plants it comes from, and the second is the name of the specific species.

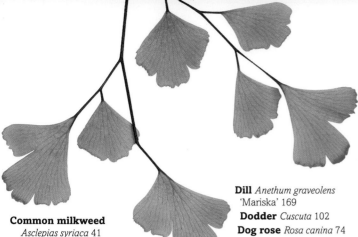

Index

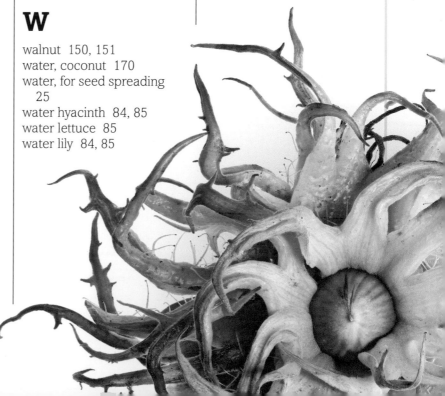

ACKNOWLEDGMENTS

The publisher would like to thank the following people for their help with making the book: Ann Baggaley, Shatarupa Chaudhari, Andrew Korah, Sarah MacCleod, Sai Prasanna, Isha Sharma, Mark Silas, and Fleur Star for editorial assistance; Noopur Dalal, Vidushi Gupta, Nidhi Mehra, and Nidhi Rastogi for design assistance; Nimesh Agrawal for picture research assistance; Anita Yadav for DTP assistance; Caroline Stamps for proofreading; Elizabeth Wise for indexing; and John Woodward for additional text.

The publisher would like to thank the following for their kind permission to reproduce their photographs:

(Key: a-above; b-below/bottom; c-centre; f-far; l-left; r-right; t-top)

123RF.com: Annieeagle 157cb, Ariadna126 78cb, Zvonimir Atletic 57tl, Atm2003 167crb, Bbtreesubmission 130cb, Belchonock 166c (Wasabi sauce), 175cl, Maksym Bondarchuk 111clb, Martin Damen 117tr, Yaroslav Domnitsky 24cb, 25tr (Milk Thistle), Easterbunnyuk 175cr (Scrub), Richard Griffin 80cb, Steven Heap 16l, Alfred Hofer 126bl, Ruttawee Jaigunta 100bc, Joemat 167cr, Natthakan Jommanee 150c, Venus Kaewyoo 1, 36–37t, Karandaev 170cr, Suradech Kongkiatpaiboon 131bl, Koosen 22ca (Sunflower seeds), Vita Kosova 143r, Magone 138c, Maksym Narodenko 135ca, 138cb, Noppharat Manakul 154tl, Angel Luis Simon Martin 142crb (Green Almonds), Andrey Milkin 131r, Pusit nimnakorn 149tr, olegdudko 134ca (Kiwi), PaylessImages 149cr, Puripat penpun 57tc, pierivb 127crb, Teera Pittayanurak 170bc (Coconut tree), D rebha 166crb, rook76 176cla, Natalie Ruffing 111c, David Schliepp 22cla, Alfio Scisetti 76cla, SHS PHOTOGRAPHY 109br, Andrey Shupilo 17br, Genadijs Stirans 151cl, Phadungsak Suphorn 131cl, Nanthawan Suwanthong 6br, 169tl, Dmitriy Syechin 113tr, Poramet Thathong 149ca, Oksana Tkachuk 101cra, utima 135tr, Phong Giap Van 151cb, Bjoern Wylezich 149crb, Svetlana Yefimkina 37crb, Yurakp 139cl (Strawberries), Иван Ульяновский 10cra (Clubmoss), 47cr (Clubmoss); **Alamy Stock Photo:** RosaIreneBetancourt 7 60cr, AB Historic 179cb, Afripics 22cb, All Canada Photos 70cra, 122c, Archive PL 48cb, Arco Images GmbH 25tr, 101tr, Arterra Picture Library 6tr, 25ca, 104ca, Bill Lea / Dembinsky Photo Associates 123r, Bruce Montagne / Dembinsky Photo Associates 36crb, Auscape International Pty Ltd 60cl, Avalon / Photoshot License 24bl, 58c, 107c, Steven Bade 161tc, Robert Biedermann 87c, Biosphoto 100–101t, 102clb, Blickwinkel 48cr, 49crb, 53tl, 75cb, 79crb, 87br, 185tl, Joe Blossom 69cla, Sebastien Bonaime 5bc, 116cb, 186–187b, Mark Boulton 111tc, Buiten-Beeld 15cb (Kapok Tree), Nigel Cattlin 20–21b, 28cb, 47crb, 87cr, 127cb, Robert Clare 101tl, Jim Clark 122cr, Mark Collinson 41bl, Collpicto 52ca, Connection One 118clb, Rob Crandall 104c, 184bl, Custom Life Science Images 41cra, Jolanta Dąbrowska 48clb, 131l, Ethan Daniels 25cl, Universal Images Group North America LLC / DeAgostini 27tl, 92c, 128cra, Danita Delimont 91cra, Douglas Peebles Photography 91crb, Joel Douillet 75tc, 185cr, Stuart Fawbert 53cb, Florapix 60clb, 78clb, Flowers and Gardens by Jan Smith Photography 113cb, Shawn Hempel - Food 131ca, Frans Lanting Studio 119tl, Stephen French 78r, Tim Gainey 86br, Bob Gibbons 59r, 60clb (Outeniqua Yellowwood), 102cb (Ivy Broomrape), 105tl, James Hackland 83r, Peter J. Hatcher 25crb, Urs Hauenstein 79tc, David Hayes 78cla, Hemis 171crb, Heritage Image Partnership Ltd 178bl, HHelene 43bc, Historic Images 179bl, Thomas Kyhn Rovsing Hjørnet 87bl, Friedrich von Hörsten 79cb, D. Hurst 179cra, Rachel Husband 138ca, imageBROKER 28bc, 59c, 68cla, 73bc, 93cr, 105tc, 110cb, 120–121, imageBROKER / Guenter Fischer 71l, Johner Images 81crb, Kyselova Inna 153c, Interfoto 167c, blickwinkel / Jagel 60cb, 100c, Juniors Bildarchiv GmbH 100cr, Steven J. Kazlowski 92clb, Tamara Kulikova 36cla, Andrii Kutsenko 176cb (Hibiscus), Hervé Lenain 113c, Shih-Hao Liao 117cla, Pete Oxford / Nature Picture Library 18–19, Steve Gschmeissner / Science Photo Library 42bc, Margery Maskell 46–47bc, mauritius images GmbH 82bl, 108–109t, 117cr, Buddy Mays 152bl, MCLA Collection 170bc, McPhoto 23c 156cla, Melba Photo Agency 26cla, MNS Photo 166cla, Jerome Moreaux 166cb, Hilary Morgan 178c, Robert Murray 81cb, Irina Naoumova 59ca, Jatesada Natayo 78c, National Geographic Image Collection 15ca, 119ca, Natural Visions 123bc, Nature Photographers Ltd 70bc, Nature Photographers Ltd / Paul R. Sterry 113clb, blickwinkel / McPHOTO / NBT 61c, Neftali 177tr, SK Hasan Ali / Alamy Live News 157tl, Dean Nixon 41bc, NPS Photo 105tr, Jose Okolo 105crb, Onehundred Percent 81bl, George Ostertag 11ca, 103tc, 112crb, 113ca, Panther Media GmbH 76bc, 87bc, Picture Partners 101c, Stefano Paterna 101cr, James Peake 71br, Thomas David Pinzer 78crb, Premium Stock Photography GmbH 117c, Steve Pridgeon 102c, Reda & Co Srl 52cb, Ian Redding 161cb, George Reszeter 25cb, RF Company 129bl, robertharding / Jack Jackson 164–165b, RZAF_Images 40c, Kjell Sandved 176ca, David Sewell 24tl, shapencolour 95cb, Shoot Froot 142crb, Antonio Siwiak 76ca, Southeast asia 103crb, Inga Spence 144tr, 188tr, Steve Allen Travel Photography 40l, Hans Stuessi 22ca (Balloon plant), 22ca (Marigold Seed), 22ca (Seed), Phillip Thomas 107cra, Travelstock44 91cr, Colin Varndell 83bl, Tom Viggars 80l, 81r, Dave Watts 68crb, 183bl, Jonny White 176clb, Wildlife GmbH 6tc, 10cla, 10fcla, 56, 57bl, 58ca, 59tl, 83cra, 101crb, 154ca, Michael Willis 103l, Robert Wyatt 76cr, Zoonar GmbH 111crb; **Barcroft Studios:** Mark Graves / Oregonian Media Group 158–159; **Keith Bradley:** 119cb; **Depositphotos**

Inc: AgaveStudio 157ca, Ajafoto 143crb, Antpkr 170cl, dabjola 87bc (loosestrife), Dbtale 22clb (Avocado), Kolesnikovserg 143clb, 182tr, levkro 117clb, Miiisha 139cl (Green grapevine), msk_nina| 5tr, 138tr, Photomaru 142ca, Sumners 174cb (Perfume), Nadja_77.Tut.by 155r, vvoennyy 33clb, ZlataMarka 130cra; **John Doebley:** Hugh Iltis, from John Doebley's image gallery 164cl; **Dorling Kindersley:** Mark Winwood / Hampton Court Flower Show 2014 74cr, Colin Keates / Natural History Museum, London 51br, Gary Ombler: Green and Gorgeous Flower Farm 169tr, Frome & District Agricultural Society 134crb, Gary Ombler / Royal Botanic Gardens, Kew 11fcla, Jeremy Gray 12cb, Josef Hlasek 49br, Frank Greenaway / Natural History Museum, London 69cl, Mark Winwood / Downderry Nursery 177cb, Peter Anderson / RHS 124–125c, Will Heap / Mike Rose 124tc, 182bl, Gary Ombler / Centre for Wildlife Gardening / London Wildlife Trust 2–3, 32crb, 40br, 80–81c, 106c, Wildlife Gardening / London Wildlife Trust 75cr, Will Heap / John Armitage 125tr, 189br, Justyn Willsmore 110l, Mark Winwood / RHS Wisley 120cb, 122bl; **Dreamstime.com:** 37704963 167cb, Tatyana Abramovich 24cl, Airubon 177crb, 183tr, Akiyoko74 154c, Natalya Aksenova 166bl, Akwitps 170cb, Alex7370 110–111cb, Alexan24 77bl, Alexfiodorov 21crb (Bean), Alessio Cola / Alexandra 139crb, Anne Amphlett 11br, Nadezhda Andriyakhina 136ca, Arkadyr 26ca, Atman 35cra, 161r, Aurinko 130bc, Natalia Bachkova 29cl, Banprik 147clb, Barmalini 94–95c, 154tr, Beatricesirinun 71cb, Barbro Bergfeldt 167cl (Vanilla), Kateryna Bibro 137cr, 149clb, Harald Biebel 117ca, Vladimir Blinov 128ca, Stephan Bock 137c, Bombaert 41br, Pichest Boonpanchua 149clb (Korean melon), 156ca, Alena Brozova 134ca, Charles Brutlag 21crb (Seed), Marc Bruxelle 32cr, 74tr, 124cb, Leonello Calvetti 42–43c, Chernetskaya 22cl, Yutthana Choradet 161clb, Mohammed Anwarul Kabir Choudhury 166cl (Sesame), 174ca, Su Chun 67tr, Sharon Cobo 7tr, 125crb, Countrymania 148cra, Cpaulfell 41ca, Cynoclub 85cl, Jolanta Dabrowska 116tr, 166c, 186tl, Denira777 145tl, 161tl, Dewins 32clb, Dianazh 175tr, Digitalimagined 35c, 48br, 49c, 60crb, Cristina Dini 174cra, Anton Ignatenco / Dionisvera 150cl, Le Thuy Do 116clb, 148–149tc, Dohnal 130br, 131br, Draftmode 23cl, 134cr (Banana), 146tl, 157cl, Reza Ebrahimi 57crb, Ed8563 59ca (Tamarack Trees), Ekays 33cl, Emilio100 143tl, 179c, Empire331 12crb, Eyeblink 15tc, Ama F 107bl, Fibobjects 77br, Sergii Koval / Fomaa 136bl, Gaja 16–17cla, Natalia Garmasheva 48ca, Patrick Gosling 122cla, Gow927 170–171c, Antonio Gravante 106tl, 171crb (Wine cork), Richard Griffin 80cra, David Hayes 69crb, Artem Honchariuk 130c, Zeng Hu 11bl, Boonchuay Iamsumang 147cb, Andrii Iarygin 13, Anton Ignatenco 150cla, Artem Illarionov 22c (Peach stone), Imagoinsulae 59clb, Irabel8 32cla, Irinaroibu 151crb, Irochka 77cla, Roman Ivaschenko 77bc, Wasana Jaigunta 128bc, 147cr, Janecat11 35clb, Jfanchin 34crb, Jianghongyan 139cl, 147c, Justas Jaru?evi?ius / Jjustas 22clb, Johannesk 118cb, Ang Wee Heng John | 12cb, Joophoek 176crb, Jpldesigns 32–33t, Numpon Jumroonsiri 24cl (Lotus seeds), Karelgallas 95cb, Katerina Kovaleva / Kkovaleva 148cr, Kav777 109clb (Tree), Kazakovmaksim 32ca, Kenishirotie 134cr, Kenmind76 135tl (pear), Khunaspix 171cl, Liliia Khuzhakhmetova 171br, Kianlin 137ca, Sharon Kingston 26crb, Klickmr 166cl, Sergey Kolesnikov 145cl, Kooslin 171cr (Hemp rope), Kostiuchenko 29tl, 29tl (flower), 29tl (poppy), Tetiana Kovalenko 104l, 175tl, Lev Kropotov 111cb, 175clb, Anna Kucherova 136cr, Tamara Kulikova 117cb, 138crb, Wipark Kulnirandorn 106crb, Kurapy11 151tr, Andrey Kurguzov 145clb, Denys Kurylow 58cb, 109cb (Evergreen Tree), Yauheni Labanau 7tc, 94cla, Kateryna Larina 107tl, Muriel Lasure 43cb, Robert Lerich 148cla, Lesichkadesign 109clb (Leaf), 154bc, Sergei Levashov 30–31c, Lightzoom 157tl (Brush), Liligraphie 153tl, Lirtlon 178crb, Luckyphotographer 91tr, Ludoriri 116crb, Thomas Lukassek 86b, Natthapon M 171clb, Robyn Mackenzie 66tc, Mahira 142crb (Almond), 166ca, Goncharuk Maksym 144clb (Red blood orange), Maocheng 157crb, Sarah Marchant 148ca, Massman 135br, Josip Matanovic 94cb, Vivian Mcaleavey 152cla, Nicola Messana 92cla, Microstock77 171cra, Barbara Delgado-millea 5bl, 144clb, Miraswonderland 34clb, Maksim Mironov 102cr, Elena Moiseeva 154cl, Graham Monamy 99bc, Tanakorn Moolsarn 171tr, Ruud Morijn 129cr, Msnobody 108ca, Tatiana Muslimova 142clb (Mango), N Van D / Nataliavand 29r, Natika 134clb, David Cabrera Navarro 166c (Tahini), Nbvf 152c, Neirfy 28br, Pedro Turrini Neto 22c, Nevinates 135clb, 146c (Persimmon), Niceregionpics 146clb, Natthawut Nungensanthia 130cb (Sorghum), Omidiii 142tr, Tatsuya Otsuka 116cla, Ovydyborets 35crb, 171cr, Palex6 145tr, Nipaporn Panyacharoen 175cb (Aloe vera), Bidouze St�phane 109crb (Rainforest), Photographieundmehr 138cla, 168cl, 169br, Photographyfirm 160cb, Anna Kucherova / Photomaru 169bc, Pikkystock 66crb, Pinkomelet 33cb, Chanwit Pinpart 94c, Pipa100 57tr, 137cb (Oca), 145crb, 149cl, 153cr, 156cra, 190tl, Pixbox77 171tc, Pixelife 25clb, Planctonvideo 127cra, Andrii Pohranychnyi 175cb, Olga Popova 49cla, Saran Poroong 38–39, Ppy2010ha 116ca, Anastasiia Prokofyeva 22crb (Dicot), Artapom Puthikampol 66tl, Ra3rn 28ca, Radu Borcoman / Radukan 49ca, Rawlik 107r, Somphop Ruksutakarn 147cb, Sergey Rybin 48bl, Thongchai Saisanguanwong 177tl, Roman Samokhin 144cl, Juana Maria Gonzalez Santos 177cr, Sarah2 43cra, Antonio Scarpi 155cl, 189tr, Bernd Schmidt 124cla, 125cr, 125cb, Martin Schneiter 92cra, Alfio Scisetti 116c, 168crb, 175crb, Eleonora Scordo 37tr, Sally Scott 135bc, 160cl, Anna Sedneva 135tl, 152–153b, Toshihisa Shimoda 86cla, 160c

(Cardoon), Alexander Sidyakov 122cra, Sirfujiyama 70tr, Poravute Siriphiroon 10br, Slallison 137cb, Sommai Sommai 145ca, 145cr, Stock Image Factory 174c, Stocksnapper 130c (Oats), Subbotina 147cb, Likit Supasai 148clb, Yodsawaj Suriyasirisin 142c, Swkunst 142tl, Taitai6769 22cr, Taechit Tanantornanutra 118cb (Fern), Maxim Tatarinov 138clb, Wallop Thamsuaydee 6tl, 146cra, 187tr, Threeart 30clb, Thungsarnphoto 171cb, Sergii Trofymchuk 28c, Ievgenii Tryfonov 109tr, Twoellis 160br, Valentyn75 7bl, 22ca (Poppy seeds), 147ca, Verastuchelova 84br, 168bc, Gabriel Vergani 131cr, Vitoriaholdingsllc 176cb, Vladvitek 23r, Vvoevale 33cla, Jürgen Wackenhut 74cl, Yael Weiss 22ca (Magnifying glass), Shane White 43crb, Yutthasart Yanakornsiri 170cb (Rope), Yvdavyd 138cr, 151ca, Zakri2023 160tr, Dzmitry Zelianeuski 112cla, Sheng Zhang 139cl (Red bayberry), Zigzagmtart 148crb, Сергей Кучугурный 150ca; **flickr.com/photos/laajala/:** 70cl; **Nigel Forshaw:** 104cla; **GAP Photos:** Jonathan Buckley 105c, Clive Nichols 113cl, Nova Photo Graphik 104cra, Friedrich Strauss 116cr, Visions 99crb; **Garden World Images:** Rita Coates 53tr; **The Garden Collection:** FP / BIOSPHOTO 99clb; **Getty Images:** 500Px Plus / Danny Dungo 72–73, Kazuo Ogawa / Aflo 71tr, AFP / Chaideer Mahyuddin 172–173, Nikolay Doychinov / Afp 75tl, AWL Images / Getty Images Plus / Catherina Unger 94clb, P. Bonduel 26cra, Corbis / Getty Images Plus / Paul Starosta 51tr, Corbis Documentary / Paul Starosta 85cr, 98clb, Creativ Studio Heinemann 138cl, De Agostini Picture Library 103tl, DEA / ARCHIVIO B / De Agostini 52crb (Spores), DigitalVision / Tony Anderson 20cra, Clay Perry / Corbis Documentary 74–75bc, Pankaj Upadhyay / EyeEm 112–113c, FlowerPhotos / UIG 29bl, Shem Compion / Gallo Images 151c, Joel Sartore / National Geographic Image Collection 87cra, André De Kesel 99cra, Konrad Wothe / Nature Picture Library 23cb, Lindeblad, Matilda 36clb, 190br, Maximilian Stock Ltd. / Photographer's Choice 154cla, Mint Images - Art Wolfe 162–163, Mint Images - Paul Edmondson 123cla, I love Photo and Apple / Moment 70clb, Jordan Lye / Moment 8–9, Moment / Callahan Galleries 58l, Pavel Gospodinov / Moment 179br, Zen Rial / Moment 129crb, Navdeep Soni Photography 174tr, Andrey Nekrasov 85br, Micha Pawlitzki / Photodisc 78tr, Ed Reschke / Photolibrary 110tr, Piotr Naskrecki / Minden Pictures 102cb, Stephen Dalton / Minden Pictures 25tl, 68cb, REDA&CO / Universal Images Group Editorial 106cb, James Morgan / robertharding 160cla, Paul Starosta 75tr, Manuel Sulzer 77ca, Yuri Smityuk\TASS 68tr, Tiler84 111r, TimArbaev 170br (Latex), Universal Images Group / Auscape 95tl, David Lees / Corbis / VCG 178cb, Visuals Unlimited / Dr. Ken Wagner 41cl, Visuals Unlimited / Henry Robison 10cra, Buddhika Weerasinghe 167clb, Woraput / E+ 125tc; **https://www.flickr.com/photos/heinerc/:** 71cr; **iStockphoto.com:** abriendomundo 96–97, Tamonwan Amornpornhaemahiran 107tr, anatchant 146c, Anna39 61tl, AntiMartina 122br, asiafoto 69c, Balky79 61cr, Ballycroy 122bc, Baramyou0708 118tl, Chengyuzheng 155cl (Mung bean), 161cl, Creativeye99 150crb, 151cr, 154cr, cristaltran 132–133, Dafinchi 104–105bc, Damocean 88–89, design56 146crb, 191cla, DigiTrees 116ca, 116cl, DmitriyKazitsyn 109cb, DrPAS 117c, Eloi_Omella 140–141, Elpy 22ca, emer1940 100crb, Enviromantic 166cr, Eyepark 119tr, fcafotodigital / E+ 160c, Floortje 100crc, fotogaby / E+ 62–63, Griffin82 82–83c, joloei 147tr, Kynny 117br, lindarocks 107cla, lnzyx 112cb, lovelyday12 118r, malerapaso 67crb, Masuti 130l, Mickey_55 176c, Mikespics 178cl, milanfoto 152cra, Natefeldman 155tc, Ninell_Art 82bc, Only_Fabrizio 142clb, PicturePartners 157clb, Pittapitta 174l, Ploychan 93ca, Portogas-D-Ace 147l, Rvimages 131bc, Sieboldianus 93r, 111tl, Sunnybeach 142cl, Tacojim 123bl, tiler84 11cb, Toktak_Kondesign 40cr, UrosPoteko 155clb, Wushoung Wang 27clb, zlikovec 109crb; © **Jeremy Rolfe (CC BY):** 80ca; **Jonas Dupuich/Bonsai Tonight:** 124c; **Farhad Karami:** 21br; **James Kuether:** 54–55; **Mary Evans Picture Library:** Library of Congress 124clb; **Jim Mercer:** 93cb; **Susan Middleton:** Photo by D. Liittschwager and S. Middleton. © 2000 76cb; **Monterey Bay Nursery:** Luen Miller 52cb (Carrot Fern); **NASA:** Kennedy Space Center 180–181, Marshall Space Flight Center 74cb; **National Geographic Creative:** Michael Nichols 114–115; **naturepl.com:** Miles Barton 83cl, Simon Colmer 94ca, Adrian Davies 34cla, 98cla, Chris Mattison 82br, 118c, MYN / Marko Masterl 100cla, Niall Benvie / MYN 48br, 53bl, Colin Varndell 48cl; **pflanzio.com:** 53cla; **Photo by Bryan Laughland:** 61tr; **PhytoImages:** Dr. Daniel L. Nickrent 102crb, 189br; **Rex by Shutterstock:** imageBROKER 93cla, Jspix / imageBROKER 70crb, Frederik / imageBROKER / Shutterstock 110ca; **Science Photo Library:** Dr Keith Wheeler 15cb, Dr Morley Read 44–45, Eye Of Science 40ca, Michael P. Gadomski 59tc, Karl Gaff 49cb, Bob Gibbons 58cr, Steve Gschmeissner 28cb (Poppy seedling), M P Land 95tc, Cordelia Molloy 69clb, John Serrao 61clb, Nigel Cattlin / Science Source 47cra, Merlin D. Tuttle 69tr; **Jenn Sinasac:** https :// www.flickr.com / jennsinasac 25cr (Used Thrice on the spread); **Rituraj Singh:** 176cra; **SuperStock:** Age Fotostock K22-216517 47cr, Biosphoto 27r, 85c, 112ca, Eye Ubiquitous 14–15c, J M Barres / age fotostock 58crb, Juniors 84cr; **Wellcome Collection http://creativecommons.org/licenses/by/4.0/:** Science Museum, London 49cra

All other images © Dorling Kindersley
For further information see: **www.dkimages.com**